AI4 Corporations
Volume I

The Corporate AI Compliance
Blueprint

Jamie Culican

Melle Melkumian

Published by Dragon Realm Press

Cape May Court House, New Jersey, USA

www.dragonrealmpress.com

AI-Enabled Technology was utilized in collaboration when creating this series.

Printed in the USA

First Edition: May 4, 2023

CONTENTS

INTRODUCTION

WELCOME TO "THE AI4 CORPORATE COMPLIANCE"! AS THE integration of artificial intelligence (AI) and machine learning technologies continues to rapidly transform industries across the globe, the importance of developing robust and comprehensive AI compliance policies has become paramount. This book has been crafted as an essential guide for organizations seeking to navigate the complex landscape of AI ethics, regulations, and best practices, while ensuring alignment with their unique goals and objectives.

In today's increasingly digital world, AI has become an indispensable tool for businesses of all sizes, enhancing efficiency, enabling innovation, and driving growth. However, with these immense benefits come new challenges and responsibilities. As such, it is crucial for organizations to proactively manage potential risks and ensure adherence to a diverse array of legal, ethical, and industry-specific standards. This comprehensive guide will walk you through the process of crafting, implementing, and refining AI Corporate Compliance Policies that reflect your organization's values and strategic vision, while effectively addressing the unique challenges that AI technologies present.

Throughout the course of this book, you will gain a deep understanding of the foundations and principles of AI compliance, as well as valuable insights into assessing your organization's needs and objectives. By leveraging the guidance provided in these pages, you will be equipped to create a tailored AI Corporate Compliance Policy that effectively integrates key principles, industry regulations, and risk mitigation strategies. Furthermore, you will explore the practical aspects of policy implementation and enforcement, fostering a culture of AI compliance, and addressing legal and ethical considerations associated with AI deployment.

To ensure that your organization remains ahead of the curve, this book also delves into the future of AI compliance, offering guidance on adapting to emerging technologies and regulations, collaborating with industry experts and regulators, and leveraging AI itself to enhance compliance management. Finally, a collection of real-world case studies will provide you with valuable examples of successful AI Corporate Compliance Policies, shedding light on best practices and unique organizational contexts.

Whether you are a seasoned AI professional, a business leader, or a compliance officer, this book is designed to empower you in navigating the intricacies of AI compliance, with the ultimate goal of driving your organization's success in the age of artificial intelligence. Together, let us embark on this exciting journey towards a more ethical, responsible, and compliant AI-powered future!

The Growing Importance of AI in Businesses

In recent years, artificial intelligence (AI) has emerged as a game-changing force, revolutionizing industries and reshaping the global business landscape. The increasing prominence of AI in businesses can be attributed to its unparalleled ability to process vast amounts of data, generate insights, and enable informed decision-making at a speed and scale previously unimaginable. By harnessing the power of AI, organizations across sectors have achieved new levels of efficiency, productivity, and competitiveness, making it an indispensable tool in today's increasingly digital world.

One of the most significant drivers of AI adoption in business is the potential for cost savings and enhanced operational efficiency. By automating routine and repetitive tasks, AI-powered systems can free up employees to focus on more strategic, creative, and value-adding activities. Furthermore, AI-driven predictive analytics and intelligent decision support systems can help organizations optimize resource allocation, streamline supply chains, and improve demand forecasting, ultimately leading to more effective and agile operations.

Beyond operational efficiency, AI has become a catalyst for innovation, enabling the development of novel products, services, and business models. Companies that effectively harness AI can gain a competitive edge by anticipating customer needs, personalizing offerings, and delivering exceptional experiences. Moreover, AI-powered tools such as natural language processing, computer vision, and sentiment analysis can facilitate a deeper understanding of customer behavior and preferences, thereby driving targeted marketing strategies and enhancing customer engagement.

Another critical aspect of AI's growing importance in business lies in its potential to address complex challenges and unlock new opportunities. For example, AI can play a significant role in enhancing cybersecurity through advanced threat detection and response, analyzing data patterns to uncover hidden risks, and predicting potential vulnerabilities. Similarly, AI can be leveraged to address pressing global concerns such as climate change and sustainability, by optimizing energy usage, reducing waste, and enabling more sustainable production processes.

However, with the exponential growth of AI's influence in the business world comes a corresponding increase in responsibility. Organizations must navigate an intricate web of ethical, legal, and regulatory considerations to ensure that their AI-driven initiatives are aligned with societal values and expectations. As such, the development and implementation of robust AI Corporate Compliance Policies have become essential for businesses seeking to harness the full potential of artificial intelligence, while minimizing risks and fostering trust among stakeholders.

The growing importance of AI in businesses cannot be overstated. It has transformed the way organizations operate, innovate, and compete, offering unprecedented opportunities for growth and success. Yet, along with these immense benefits comes the responsibility to address the unique challenges that AI presents. By embracing AI compliance and ethical considerations, organizations can effectively harness the power of AI while maintaining the trust and confidence of their customers, employees, and partners.

THE NEED FOR AI CORPORATE COMPLIANCE POLICIES

As the influence of artificial intelligence (AI) continues to expand in the business world, the need for comprehensive AI Corporate Compliance Policies becomes increasingly vital. These policies serve as the backbone for organizations seeking to harness the benefits of AI while effectively managing risks and ensuring alignment with legal, ethical, and industry-specific standards. By establishing a robust AI compliance framework, companies can create an environment of trust and transparency, fostering responsible innovation and safeguarding their reputations in an increasingly AI-driven landscape.

A key reason for the growing need for AI Corporate Compliance Policies is the potential for AI systems to inadvertently perpetuate bias, discrimination, and unfairness. As AI technologies often rely on data to make decisions and predictions, they can inadvertently learn and reproduce existing biases present in the data, leading to unintended consequences and ethical concerns. By implementing AI compliance policies that prioritize fairness and bias mitigation, organizations can demonstrate their commitment to upholding ethical standards and ensure that their AI solutions are inclusive and equitable.

Data privacy and protection are also critical considerations in the context of AI. With the increasing prevalence of data breaches and mounting public concern over data misuse, organizations must implement AI compliance policies that adhere to relevant data protection regulations, such as the General Data Protection Regulation (GDPR) and the California Consumer Privacy Act (CCPA). These policies should encompass guidelines for data collection, storage, and usage, as well as measures to ensure transparency and consent from stakeholders.

Furthermore, the rapidly evolving nature of AI technologies and the accompanying regulatory landscape makes it essential for organizations to develop adaptable AI Corporate Compliance Policies. Companies must remain agile and responsive to emerging regulations, industry best practices, and technological advancements, ensuring that their compliance policies remain relevant and effective in a constantly changing environment.

AI compliance policies also play a crucial role in fostering accountability and responsibility within organizations. By delineating clear roles, responsibilities, and decision-making authority, these policies can help ensure that appropriate oversight and governance mechanisms are in place. This, in turn, can aid in building trust among stakeholders, including employees, customers, and investors, as well as demonstrate a company's commitment to responsible AI deployment.

The need for AI Corporate Compliance Policies is more pressing than ever as organizations increasingly leverage AI technologies to drive growth and innovation. By proactively addressing ethical, legal, and regulatory considerations, businesses can not only mitigate potential risks but also create a foundation for responsible AI deployment that supports long-term success and fosters trust among stakeholders. With the right compliance policies in place, organizations can confidently navigate the exciting opportunities and challenges that artificial intelligence presents.

Overview of the Book's Content and Objectives

"The AI Corporate Compliance Blueprint: Crafting Customized Policies for the Future" has been designed as a comprehensive guide for organizations looking to develop, implement, and maintain effective AI compliance policies in an ever-evolving landscape. The content of this book is structured to provide you with the necessary insights, tools, and strategies to successfully navigate the complex world of AI ethics, regulations, and best practices, while ensuring alignment with your unique goals and objectives.

The book begins by delving into the foundations and principles of AI compliance, helping you to understand the core components, key ethical considerations, and the role of compliance in fostering responsible innovation. This foundational knowledge will equip you with the context and perspective required to effectively assess your organization's AI strategy, goals, and industry-specific regulations, while identifying potential risks and challenges associated with AI deployment.

As you progress through the book, you will gain valuable guidance on crafting a tailored AI Corporate Compliance Policy that effectively incorporates key principles, industry regulations, and risk mitigation strategies. You will also explore practical aspects of policy implementation and enforcement, including communication, establishing roles and responsibilities, monitoring, reporting, and continuous improvement.

In addition to addressing the practical aspects of AI compliance, the book delves into fostering a culture of AI compliance within your organization, by raising awareness, encouraging ethical decision-making, and integrating compliance into the fabric of your organization's culture. Moreover, you will navigate the legal and ethical considerations in AI deployment, such as data privacy, bias mitigation, transparency, and accountability.

As your organization's AI initiatives continue to evolve, it is essential to stay ahead of emerging risks and adapt to new technologies and regulations. This book provides guidance on risk assessment, management, and training programs to help you maintain a strong AI compliance posture. You will also learn about cross-functional collaboration, auditing, reporting, and managing AI compliance in the context of mergers, acquisitions, and partnerships.

To prepare for the future of AI compliance, the book explores adapting to emerging technologies and regulations, leveraging AI to enhance compliance management, and collaborating with industry experts and regulators. Additionally, a collection of case studies will provide you with real-world examples of successful AI Corporate Compliance Policies across various industries, offering insights into best practices and unique organizational contexts.

The primary objective of this book is to empower you to develop and maintain robust AI Corporate Compliance

Policies that drive business success while upholding ethical standards and addressing the unique challenges that AI technologies present. By embracing a proactive approach to AI compliance management and fostering a culture of responsibility, your organization can thrive in the age of artificial intelligence, while fostering trust and confidence among stakeholders.

IMPORTANCE OF CUSTOMIZATION AND ADAPTABILITY IN AI CORPORATE COMPLIANCE POLICIES

In the dynamic world of artificial intelligence, the importance of customization and adaptability in AI Corporate Compliance Policies cannot be overstated. As AI technologies continue to advance at an unprecedented pace, organizations must be prepared to navigate a diverse array of legal, ethical, and industry-specific challenges that may arise. By developing customized and adaptable AI compliance policies, companies can ensure that their approach to AI governance remains relevant, effective, and aligned with their unique goals and objectives.

Customization is crucial in AI compliance policies because each organization's AI strategy, industry context, and risk profile may differ significantly. A one-size-fits-all approach to AI compliance is unlikely to address the unique challenges and opportunities that each organization faces. By tailoring AI compliance policies to reflect specific industry regulations, organizational objectives, and internal culture, companies can create a framework that effectively mitigates risks and fosters responsible AI deployment.

For example, a financial services company may face strict regulations related to data privacy and security, while a healthcare organization might need to prioritize compliance with medical device regulations and patient confidentiality. Customizing AI compliance policies to address these industry-specific concerns can help organizations maintain regulatory compliance and avoid costly penalties, while also demonstrating a commitment to ethical AI deployment.

Adaptability is another essential component of effective AI Corporate Compliance Policies. Given the rapidly evolving nature of AI technologies and the accompanying regulatory landscape, organizations must remain agile and responsive to emerging regulations, industry best practices, and technological advancements. By building adaptability into their AI compliance policies, companies can quickly adjust their strategies and practices to respond to new developments, ensuring that their compliance policies remain relevant and effective in a constantly changing environment.

To foster adaptability, organizations should establish mechanisms for regular policy review, stakeholder feedback, and refinement. This process should involve input from a diverse array of internal and external stakeholders, including employees, legal experts, and industry regulators. By continuously evaluating and updating their AI compliance policies, companies can stay ahead of emerging risks, capitalize on new opportunities, and maintain a strong compliance posture in the face of uncertainty.

The importance of customization and adaptability in AI Corporate Compliance Policies cannot be overemphasized. By tailoring policies to address unique organizational needs and remaining responsive to the evolving AI landscape, companies can effectively manage risks, uphold ethical standards, and drive long-term success in the age of artificial intelligence.

CHAPTER 1

UNDERSTANDING AI COMPLIANCE: FOUNDATIONS AND PRINCIPLES - INTRODUCTION

As organizations increasingly integrate artificial intelligence (AI) into their operations and strategies, understanding the foundations and principles of AI compliance becomes essential for successful and responsible AI deployment. AI compliance encompasses the legal, ethical, and regulatory considerations that organizations must address to ensure that their AI-driven initiatives align with societal values, industry standards, and stakeholder expectations. By gaining a deep understanding of the core concepts and principles that underpin AI compliance, businesses can navigate the complexities of AI governance and create a solid foundation for ethical AI innovation.

The foundations of AI compliance involve a comprehensive understanding of the various components that contribute to responsible AI deployment. These components include adherence to relevant laws and regulations, ethical considerations such as fairness, transparency, and accountability, as well as industry-specific guidelines and best practices. By mastering these foundations, organizations can develop a holistic approach to AI compliance that addresses the multifaceted nature of AI governance.

The principles of AI compliance serve as the guiding values that should inform an organization's approach to AI governance. While the specific principles may vary depending on the industry, organizational context, and regulatory environment, some key principles that are widely recognized and accepted include:

1. Fairness: Ensuring that AI systems do not perpetuate bias or discrimination and that they treat all individuals and groups equitably.
2. Transparency: Providing clear, understandable explanations of how AI systems operate and make decisions, enabling stakeholders to assess the technology's trustworthiness.
3. Accountability: Establishing clear lines of responsibility and oversight for AI-driven decisions and actions, including mechanisms for addressing adverse impacts and unintended consequences.
4. Privacy: Safeguarding the confidentiality, integrity, and availability of data used in AI

systems, as well as protecting the privacy rights of individuals and organizations affected by the technology.

5. Security: Implementing robust measures to protect AI systems from unauthorized access, tampering, or exploitation, ensuring the resilience and reliability of the technology.

By grounding their AI compliance efforts in these foundational concepts and principles, organizations can create a strong, values-driven framework for AI governance that fosters responsible innovation, minimizes risks, and builds trust among stakeholders. In the following sections, we will delve deeper into these principles, explore their implications for AI deployment, and provide guidance on incorporating them into a comprehensive AI Corporate Compliance Policy.

DEFINING AI COMPLIANCE AND ITS COMPONENTS

AI compliance can be broadly defined as the adherence to legal, ethical, and regulatory standards associated with the development, deployment, and management of artificial intelligence (AI) technologies within an organization. Ensuring AI compliance is crucial for organizations to minimize risks, maintain public trust, and foster responsible innovation. By understanding the components of AI compliance, businesses can create a comprehensive framework that addresses the complexities of AI governance and supports long-term success in the age of AI.

The components of AI compliance can be categorized into the following key areas:

1. Legal and Regulatory Compliance: This component involves ensuring that an organization's AI initiatives align with applicable laws, regulations, and industry standards. Legal and regulatory compliance may encompass data protection and privacy laws, such as the General Data Protection Regulation (GDPR) and the California Consumer Privacy Act (CCPA), as well as industry-specific regulations related to AI deployment. Compliance with these legal frameworks is essential to avoid penalties, protect stakeholder interests, and demonstrate a commitment to responsible AI deployment.

2. Ethical Compliance: Ethical compliance focuses on upholding widely accepted ethical principles, such as fairness, transparency, accountability, and privacy, in the development and deployment of AI technologies. Organizations should establish guidelines and processes that help identify, mitigate, and monitor potential ethical risks associated with AI systems, such as biases,

discrimination, and unintended consequences. By prioritizing ethical compliance, businesses can ensure that their AI initiatives are aligned with societal values and stakeholder expectations.

3. Technical Compliance: Technical compliance encompasses the implementation of best practices and industry standards related to the development, deployment, and management of AI systems. This may include following established methodologies for AI system design, data management, and algorithmic fairness, as well as implementing robust security measures to protect AI systems from unauthorized access and exploitation. Technical compliance plays a crucial role in ensuring the resilience, reliability, and performance of AI technologies.

4. Organizational Compliance: Organizational compliance refers to the alignment of AI initiatives with an organization's internal policies, procedures, and culture. This may involve integrating AI compliance into corporate governance structures, fostering a culture of AI compliance among employees, and establishing clear roles and responsibilities for AI-related decision-making and oversight. By embedding AI compliance into the fabric of an organization, businesses can create an environment that

supports ethical AI deployment and continuous improvement.

5. Cross-functional Compliance: Cross-functional compliance involves the collaboration and coordination of various departments within an organization to ensure comprehensive AI compliance management. This may include engaging legal, IT, HR, and other relevant departments in the development, implementation, and monitoring of AI compliance policies and processes. Cross-functional compliance is essential for addressing the diverse array of legal, ethical, technical, and organizational challenges associated with AI deployment.

By recognizing and addressing each of these components, organizations can create a robust AI compliance framework that effectively manages risks, fosters responsible AI innovation, and builds trust among stakeholders. In the upcoming sections, we will explore these components in greater detail, providing guidance on incorporating them into a comprehensive AI Corporate Compliance Policy.

Key Principles of AI Ethics and Regulation

As artificial intelligence (AI) continues to play an increasingly prominent role in our society, organizations must prioritize ethical considerations and regulatory compliance in their AI initiatives. Adhering to key principles of AI ethics and regulation enables businesses to mitigate risks, build trust with stakeholders, and foster responsible innovation. Some of the most widely recognized principles of AI ethics and regulation, which serve as the foundation for effective AI governance, include fairness, transparency, accountability, privacy, security, and human-centric approach.

Fairness in AI involves developing and deploying AI systems that treat all individuals and groups equitably, avoiding biases and discriminatory outcomes. Organizations should strive to identify and mitigate potential biases in their AI systems, ensuring that their technologies do not perpetuate or exacerbate existing inequalities. Promoting fairness in AI can help businesses foster inclusivity, maintain public trust, and adhere to anti-discrimination laws.

Transparency is a cornerstone of AI ethics and involves providing clear and understandable explanations of how AI systems operate, make decisions, and impact users. Ensuring transparency in AI systems can enable stakeholders to assess the technology's trustworthiness, while also facilitating accountability and informed decision-making. Organizations should prioritize transparency in their AI initiatives by clearly communicating their methodologies, objectives, and potential risks associated with AI deployment.

Accountability in AI refers to the establishment of clear lines of responsibility and oversight for AI-driven decisions and actions. Organizations must be able to answer for the consequences of their AI systems, including any adverse impacts or unintended outcomes. To promote accountability, businesses should implement mechanisms for monitoring AI performance, addressing concerns, and, if necessary, providing redress to those affected by AI systems.

The principle of privacy in AI encompasses the protection of personal and sensitive data used in AI systems, as well as respecting the privacy rights of individuals and organizations. Organizations should ensure that their AI initiatives comply with data protection laws and industry standards, such as the General Data Protection Regulation (GDPR) and the California Consumer Privacy Act (CCPA). This includes implementing robust data management practices, providing transparency around data usage, and safeguarding data against unauthorized access or misuse.

Security is a critical aspect of AI ethics and regulation, as AI systems can be vulnerable to attacks, unauthorized access, or exploitation. Organizations should prioritize security in their AI initiatives by implementing robust measures to protect AI systems from potential threats, ensuring the resilience and reliability of the technology. This may involve adhering to industry best practices, establishing secure development processes, and regularly conducting security audits to identify and mitigate vulnerabilities.

A human-centric approach to AI ethics and regulation places the well-being, autonomy, and rights of individuals at the forefront of AI development and deployment. By prioritizing human values, organizations can ensure that AI technologies serve to enhance human capabilities, empower users, and promote the greater good. Adopting a human-centric approach can help businesses align their AI initiatives with societal values, stakeholder expectations, and ethical considerations, fostering responsible innovation and long-term success in the age of AI.

THE ROLE OF AI COMPLIANCE IN RESPONSIBLE INNOVATION

In today's rapidly evolving technological landscape, responsible innovation is essential for organizations seeking to harness the potential of artificial intelligence (AI) while minimizing potential risks and adverse impacts. AI compliance plays a pivotal role in fostering responsible innovation, as it ensures that AI initiatives align with legal, ethical, and regulatory standards, and adhere to the principles of fairness, transparency, accountability, privacy, and security.

Responsible innovation involves developing and deploying AI technologies that not only deliver value to organizations and their stakeholders but also promote positive societal outcomes and uphold ethical values. By prioritizing AI compliance, businesses can effectively manage the risks and challenges associated with AI development and deployment, such as biased decision-making, privacy violations, and security breaches. This, in turn, helps maintain public trust, protect stakeholder interests, and preserve the reputation of the organization.

Moreover, AI compliance is crucial in establishing a strong foundation for corporate governance in the age of AI. By integrating AI compliance into organizational processes and decision-making, businesses can ensure that their AI initiatives are guided by a robust ethical framework, which promotes accountability and transparency. This fosters a culture of responsibility, where employees and stakeholders are encouraged to consider the ethical implications of their AI-driven decisions and actions.

Furthermore, AI compliance contributes to long-term business success by facilitating continuous improvement and adaptability. By regularly monitoring, evaluating, and updating AI policies and practices, organizations can stay ahead of emerging risks, regulatory changes, and technological advancements. This proactive approach to AI compliance enables businesses to remain competitive and responsive to evolving market demands while maintaining their commitment to responsible innovation.

In conclusion, AI compliance plays an integral role in responsible innovation by ensuring that AI initiatives adhere to ethical principles, legal standards, and industry best practices. By prioritizing AI compliance, organizations can effectively navigate the complex landscape of AI development and deployment, minimize potential risks, and maximize the positive impact of AI technologies on society.

FINAL THOUGHTS

As we conclude our exploration of AI compliance and its vital role in responsible innovation, it is crucial to emphasize that the journey towards responsible AI governance is an ongoing, dynamic process. Businesses must remain vigilant and adaptable, continuously refining their AI policies and practices in response to emerging challenges, technological advancements, and evolving regulatory landscapes.

Embracing a proactive and thoughtful approach to AI compliance is essential for organizations seeking to harness the transformative power of AI while upholding ethical values, legal standards, and stakeholder expectations. By cultivating a culture of responsibility and accountability, businesses can ensure that their AI initiatives contribute to long-term success, enhance societal well-being, and foster trust among stakeholders.

Moreover, as AI technologies become increasingly sophisticated and integrated into various aspects of our lives, collaboration among organizations, policymakers, regulators, and industry experts will be crucial to address shared challenges and develop robust AI governance frameworks. Engaging in cross-sectoral dialogue and knowledge-sharing can facilitate the development of best practices, innovative solutions, and harmonized standards that promote responsible innovation across industries.

Ultimately, the future of AI holds immense promise and potential, but it is incumbent upon businesses to act as responsible stewards of these transformative technologies. By prioritizing AI compliance and embracing responsible innovation, organizations can not only drive growth and success but also contribute to the development of a more equitable, sustainable, and prosperous future for all.

CHAPTER 2

ASSESSING ORGANIZATIONAL NEEDS AND OBJECTIVES: LAYING THE GROUNDWORK FOR AI COMPLIANCE

AS ORGANIZATIONS EMBARK ON THEIR JOURNEY TO DEVELOP and implement effective AI Corporate Compliance Policies, a critical first step is to assess their unique needs and objectives. This process enables businesses to tailor their AI compliance strategies to their specific context, ensuring a strong alignment between AI initiatives and overall corporate goals. In this section, we will introduce the importance of assessing organizational needs and objectives, highlighting the key factors that must be considered to lay a solid foundation for successful AI compliance management.

EVALUATING YOUR ORGANIZATION'S AI STRATEGY AND GOALS: ALIGNING COMPLIANCE WITH BUSINESS OBJECTIVES

To effectively address AI compliance, organizations must first evaluate their existing AI strategy and goals, ensuring that these objectives are clearly defined and in line with broader business aims. A comprehensive understanding of an organization's AI initiatives can provide valuable insights into the specific compliance challenges that may arise, as well as the potential opportunities for responsible innovation. In this section, we will discuss the importance of evaluating your organization's AI strategy and goals as a crucial step in developing a robust AI Corporate Compliance Policy.

A thorough evaluation of your organization's AI strategy and goals involves identifying the key areas where AI technologies are being deployed or considered for deployment, as well as the specific use cases that these technologies are intended to address. This can include, for example, customer service automation, fraud detection, supply chain optimization, or predictive analytics. By gaining a comprehensive understanding of the organization's AI initiatives, businesses can better anticipate the compliance challenges that may emerge and develop targeted strategies to address these concerns.

Moreover, evaluating your organization's AI strategy and goals can help identify potential gaps or inconsistencies in the current approach to AI compliance. This process may reveal areas where additional resources, training, or expertise may be needed to ensure that AI initiatives are developed and implemented in a manner that is consistent with legal, ethical, and regulatory standards.

Finally, a clear understanding of your organization's AI strategy and goals can help ensure that your AI Corporate Compliance Policy is closely aligned with overall business objectives. This alignment is essential for maximizing the value of AI initiatives, fostering a culture of responsibility and accountability, and driving long-term success in the age of AI. By evaluating and refining your organization's AI strategy and goals, businesses can lay the groundwork for a robust and effective AI compliance management program that supports responsible innovation and growth.

IDENTIFYING INDUSTRY-SPECIFIC REGULATIONS AND REQUIREMENTS: NAVIGATING THE AI COMPLIANCE LANDSCAPE

A key aspect of developing a comprehensive AI Corporate Compliance Policy is identifying the industry-specific regulations and requirements that govern the use of artificial intelligence in your organization's domain. Understanding the unique legal, ethical, and regulatory frameworks that apply to your industry can help ensure that your AI initiatives comply with relevant standards and minimize the risk of non-compliance. In this section, we will discuss the importance of identifying industry-specific regulations and requirements and the role they play in shaping an organization's approach to AI compliance.

Different industries are subject to varying degrees of regulatory scrutiny, and the rules governing the use of AI can also differ significantly across sectors. For instance, organizations operating in heavily regulated industries, such as finance, healthcare, or transportation, may face a more complex compliance landscape than those in less regulated sectors. To effectively navigate this landscape, businesses must familiarize themselves with the specific regulations and requirements that apply to their industry, such as data protection laws, anti-discrimination rules, or safety standards.

Identifying industry-specific regulations and requirements involves conducting thorough research, consulting with legal experts, and staying informed about emerging regulatory developments. Organizations should also consider engaging with industry associations, regulatory bodies, and peer organizations to gain insights into best practices and evolving expectations around AI compliance in their sector.

Moreover, it is essential for businesses to recognize that the AI compliance landscape is continually evolving, as lawmakers and regulators work to keep pace with rapidly advancing technologies. Organizations must be prepared to adapt their AI Corporate Compliance Policies in response to changing regulations and requirements, ensuring that their AI initiatives remain compliant and aligned with industry standards.

Identifying industry-specific regulations and requirements is a critical step in developing a tailored AI Corporate Compliance Policy that meets the unique needs and challenges of your organization's domain. By understanding and addressing the regulatory landscape in which your business operates, you can effectively mitigate compliance risks, protect stakeholder interests, and foster responsible innovation in the age of AI.

ANALYZING POTENTIAL RISKS AND CHALLENGES IN AI DEPLOYMENT: PROACTIVE RISK MANAGEMENT FOR AI COMPLIANCE

The deployment of artificial intelligence technologies presents a variety of potential risks and challenges that organizations must carefully consider when developing their AI Corporate Compliance Policies. These risks can range from ethical concerns, such as biased decision-making and privacy violations, to operational and financial risks, such as security breaches or regulatory non-compliance. In this section, we will discuss the importance of analyzing potential risks and challenges in AI deployment as a crucial component of effective AI compliance management.

A comprehensive risk analysis involves identifying the various risks associated with your organization's AI initiatives, assessing their potential impact and likelihood, and prioritizing the most critical risks for mitigation. This process can help organizations proactively address potential challenges, minimize adverse consequences, and ensure that AI technologies are deployed in a responsible and compliant manner.

To effectively analyze potential risks and challenges in AI deployment, organizations must first develop a thorough understanding of their AI initiatives, as well as the specific industry regulations and requirements that apply to their domain. This knowledge can help businesses identify areas of potential concern, such as data privacy, algorithmic bias, or system security, and develop targeted strategies to address these risks.

Moreover, organizations should consider conducting regular AI risk assessments, which can help identify emerging risks and monitor the effectiveness of existing risk mitigation measures. These assessments can be informed by various sources, such as internal audits, external benchmarking, or stakeholder feedback, and can help ensure that AI compliance policies remain up-to-date and responsive to evolving risks and challenges.

Finally, it is essential for organizations to recognize that AI technologies are continually evolving, and the risks and challenges associated with AI deployment are likely to shift over time. By adopting a proactive and dynamic approach to risk analysis, businesses can stay ahead of emerging concerns, adapt their AI compliance policies as needed, and foster a culture of responsible innovation.

Analyzing potential risks and challenges in AI deployment is a key element of effective AI compliance management. By proactively identifying, assessing, and addressing the risks associated with AI technologies, organizations can minimize adverse impacts, protect stakeholder interests, and ensure the responsible and compliant deployment of AI solutions.

FINAL THOUGHTS

As we conclude this chapter on assessing organizational needs and objectives, it is crucial to recognize that the development of robust AI Corporate Compliance Policies requires a comprehensive and proactive approach. By evaluating your organization's AI strategy and goals, identifying industry-specific regulations and requirements, and analyzing potential risks and challenges in AI deployment, businesses can lay the groundwork for effective AI compliance management and responsible innovation.

Embracing a comprehensive approach to AI compliance is essential for organizations seeking to harness the transformative power of AI while upholding ethical values, legal standards, and stakeholder expectations. As AI technologies continue to evolve and permeate various aspects of our lives, businesses must remain vigilant and adaptable, continuously refining their AI policies and practices in response to emerging challenges and regulatory developments.

Moreover, fostering a culture of AI compliance within

the organization is key to ensuring that employees at all levels understand and embrace the importance of responsible AI deployment. By cultivating a shared commitment to AI compliance and providing the necessary resources, training, and support, organizations can ensure that their AI initiatives contribute to long-term success, enhance societal well-being, and foster trust among stakeholders.

Finally, collaboration among organizations, policymakers, regulators, and industry experts is crucial to addressing shared challenges and developing robust AI governance frameworks. Engaging in cross-sectoral dialogue and knowledge-sharing can facilitate the development of best practices, innovative solutions, and harmonized standards that promote responsible innovation across industries.

In summary, the journey towards responsible AI governance is an ongoing, dynamic process that requires organizations to embrace a comprehensive approach to AI compliance management. By prioritizing AI compliance and adapting to the evolving AI landscape, businesses can not only drive growth and success but also contribute to the development of a more equitable, sustainable, and prosperous future for all.

CHAPTER 3

CRAFTING A TAILORED AI CORPORATE COMPLIANCE POLICY: DESIGNING A CUSTOMIZED ROADMAP FOR RESPONSIBLE AI DEPLOYMENT

IN AN ERA MARKED BY RAPID ADVANCEMENTS IN ARTIFICIAL intelligence, organizations must recognize the importance of crafting a tailored AI Corporate Compliance Policy that addresses their unique needs and challenges. A customized policy can not only help businesses navigate the complex landscape of AI compliance but also ensure that AI initiatives are aligned with organizational goals and ethical principles. In this section, we will introduce the concept of crafting a tailored AI Corporate Compliance Policy, emphasizing the benefits of developing a customized roadmap for responsible AI deployment in your organization.

A well-designed AI Corporate Compliance Policy serves as a comprehensive guide for organizations, outlining the key principles, processes, and practices that govern the development, deployment, and management of AI technologies.

By customizing this policy to reflect the specific needs and objectives of your organization, you can ensure that AI initiatives are developed and implemented in a manner that is consistent with legal, ethical, and regulatory standards, as well as aligned with your organization's culture and values.

Crafting a tailored AI Corporate Compliance Policy requires organizations to take a deep dive into their AI strategy and goals, industry-specific regulations and requirements, and potential risks and challenges associated with AI deployment. This process enables businesses to identify the key components and considerations that should be incorporated into their policy, ensuring a strong alignment between AI initiatives and overall corporate goals.

Moreover, developing a customized AI Corporate Compliance Policy can help organizations foster a culture of AI compliance, empowering employees at all levels to understand and embrace the importance of responsible AI deployment. By providing clear guidance on the roles and responsibilities of various stakeholders, as well as the tools and resources needed for effective AI compliance management, a tailored policy can help drive a shared commitment to responsible innovation.

In summary, crafting a tailored AI Corporate Compliance Policy is a critical step in ensuring that your organization's AI initiatives are developed and deployed in a responsible and compliant manner. By designing a customized roadmap for AI compliance that reflects the unique needs and objectives of your organization, you can effectively navigate the complex landscape of AI governance, foster a culture of responsibility, and harness the power of AI to drive long-term success.

DEVELOPING A POLICY FRAMEWORK AND STRUCTURE: BUILDING THE FOUNDATION FOR EFFECTIVE AI COMPLIANCE MANAGEMENT

A crucial aspect of crafting a tailored AI Corporate Compliance Policy is the development of a comprehensive policy framework and structure that outlines the guiding principles, processes, and practices governing AI initiatives within your organization. A well-defined framework and structure can help provide clarity, consistency, and direction, enabling organizations to effectively manage AI compliance and foster a culture of responsible innovation. In this section, we will discuss the importance of developing a policy framework and structure, along with key considerations for building a solid foundation for effective AI compliance management.

Developing a policy framework and structure involves establishing a coherent set of guiding principles, objectives, and processes that serve as the foundation for your AI Corporate Compliance Policy. These guiding principles should be based on industry-specific regulations, ethical considerations, and organizational values, ensuring that your policy is aligned with both external and internal expectations.

The policy framework should also address key aspects of AI compliance management, such as roles and responsibilities, risk assessment and mitigation, monitoring and reporting, and continuous improvement. By clearly defining these elements within the policy framework, organizations can ensure that employees and stakeholders have a clear understanding of their responsibilities and expectations in relation to AI compliance.

In designing the structure of your AI Corporate Compliance Policy, it is essential to ensure that the policy is organized in a clear, logical, and easily accessible manner. This may involve breaking down the policy into distinct sections or chapters, each addressing a specific aspect of AI compliance management. The structure should be designed in a way that allows for easy navigation, quick reference, and seamless integration of new information as regulations, technologies, and organizational needs evolve.

Developing a comprehensive policy framework and structure is a critical step in crafting a tailored AI Corporate Compliance Policy that effectively addresses the unique needs and objectives of your organization. By establishing a solid foundation based on guiding principles, objectives, and processes, organizations can successfully navigate the complex landscape of AI compliance and drive a culture of responsible innovation.

INCORPORATING KEY PRINCIPLES AND INDUSTRY REGULATIONS: ENSURING COMPLIANCE AND ETHICAL AI DEPLOYMENT

A cornerstone of an effective AI Corporate Compliance Policy is the incorporation of key principles and industry regulations that govern the development, deployment, and management of AI technologies. By embedding these principles and regulations within your policy, you can ensure that your organization's AI initiatives adhere to legal, ethical, and regulatory standards, and contribute to the responsible innovation of AI technologies. In this section, we will discuss the importance of incorporating key principles and industry regulations into your AI Corporate Compliance Policy, and the steps organizations can take to achieve this objective.

Key principles related to AI ethics and compliance generally include transparency, fairness, accountability, privacy, and security. These principles serve as the foundation for responsible AI deployment, and integrating them into your policy can help ensure that AI technologies are developed and implemented in a manner that respects human rights, upholds legal standards, and fosters trust among stakeholders.

Incorporating industry regulations into your AI Corporate Compliance Policy involves identifying the specific legal requirements and standards that apply to your organization's domain, such as data protection laws, anti-discrimination regulations, or industry-specific guidelines for AI deployment. These regulations can vary depending on the jurisdiction, sector, or use case, and it is essential for organizations to stay abreast of the latest regulatory developments and ensure their policy remains up-to-date and compliant.

To successfully incorporate key principles and industry regulations into your AI Corporate Compliance Policy, organizations should start by conducting a thorough review of the relevant laws, standards, and best practices that govern AI deployment in their industry. This may involve consulting with legal experts, industry bodies, or regulators to gain a comprehensive understanding of the applicable requirements and expectations.

Once these principles and regulations have been identified, organizations should embed them within the policy framework, ensuring that they are integrated into the various processes, practices, and decision-making procedures related to AI compliance management. This may involve developing specific guidelines or checklists that help employees and stakeholders adhere to the key principles and industry regulations, as well as establishing monitoring and reporting mechanisms to ensure ongoing compliance.

Incorporating key principles and industry regulations into your AI Corporate Compliance Policy is crucial for ensuring that your organization's AI initiatives adhere to legal, ethical, and regulatory standards, and contribute to the responsible innovation of AI technologies. By embedding these principles and regulations within your policy, you can foster a culture of AI compliance, protect stakeholder interests, and drive long-term success in the age of AI.

ADDRESSING POTENTIAL RISKS AND MITIGATION STRATEGIES: PROACTIVELY MANAGING AI-RELATED CHALLENGES

A key component of a comprehensive AI Corporate Compliance Policy is the identification and management of potential risks associated with AI deployment, as well as the development of effective mitigation strategies. By proactively addressing these risks and challenges, organizations can ensure that their AI initiatives are implemented responsibly, and potential negative consequences are minimized or avoided. In this section, we will discuss the importance of addressing potential risks and mitigation strategies in your AI Corporate Compliance Policy, and provide guidance on how organizations can effectively manage AI-related challenges.

AI technologies, while offering numerous benefits and opportunities for businesses, can also present risks in areas such as data privacy, security, bias, transparency, and accountability. These risks can have serious implications for organizations, potentially leading to legal penalties, reputational damage, or loss of trust among stakeholders. As a result, it is essential for organizations to proactively identify and address these risks within their AI Corporate Compliance Policy.

To effectively manage AI-related risks, organizations should start by conducting a comprehensive risk assessment that identifies the potential hazards associated with the development, deployment, and management of AI technologies. This assessment should consider both the likelihood and impact of each risk, and prioritize those that pose the greatest threat to the organization's objectives, stakeholders, or regulatory compliance.

Once potential risks have been identified, organizations should develop and incorporate mitigation strategies within their AI Corporate Compliance Policy. These strategies may include implementing robust data protection measures, developing transparent algorithms, adopting explainable AI techniques, or establishing clear lines of accountability for AI decision-making. By outlining these mitigation strategies within the policy, organizations can provide employees and stakeholders with clear guidance on how to prevent, minimize, or manage AI-related risks.

In addition to developing mitigation strategies, organizations should establish mechanisms for monitoring and reporting on AI-related risks, as well as for continuously improving their risk management practices. This may involve setting up regular risk assessment processes, reporting requirements, and feedback loops that enable the organization to stay ahead of emerging risks and refine its mitigation strategies as needed.

Addressing potential risks and mitigation strategies in your AI Corporate Compliance Policy is crucial for ensuring that your organization's AI initiatives are implemented responsibly and potential negative consequences are minimized or avoided. By proactively identifying and managing AI-related challenges, organizations can foster a culture of AI compliance, protect stakeholder interests, and drive long-term success in the age of AI.

ALIGNING THE POLICY WITH ORGANIZATIONAL OBJECTIVES AND CULTURE: CREATING SYNERGY BETWEEN AI COMPLIANCE AND BUSINESS SUCCESS

A critical factor in the success of an AI Corporate Compliance Policy is its alignment with organizational objectives and culture. By ensuring that your policy supports your organization's strategic goals and reinforces its core values, you can create a cohesive, supportive environment that facilitates responsible AI deployment and drives business success. In this section, we will discuss the importance of aligning your AI Corporate Compliance Policy with organizational objectives and culture, and provide guidance on how to achieve this alignment effectively.

Aligning your AI Corporate Compliance Policy with organizational objectives involves ensuring that the policy supports and contributes to the achievement of your organization's strategic goals, such as improving operational efficiency, enhancing customer experiences, or driving innovation. By incorporating these objectives into the policy, you can demonstrate how AI compliance is not only a legal and ethical responsibility but also a key driver of business success.

To align your policy with organizational objectives, it is essential to engage with senior leadership, business units, and other key stakeholders to understand their strategic goals, priorities, and concerns related to AI deployment. This engagement should inform the development of the policy framework and structure, as well as the specific processes, practices, and decision-making procedures related to AI compliance management.

In addition to aligning your AI Corporate Compliance Policy with organizational objectives, it is equally important to ensure that the policy is compatible with and reinforces your organization's culture. This involves integrating the core values, beliefs, and norms that characterize your organization's identity into the policy, and fostering a culture of AI compliance that is consistent with these cultural attributes.

To achieve this cultural alignment, organizations should ensure that the policy is communicated effectively to employees and stakeholders, using language and messaging that resonate with the organization's cultural values. Moreover, the policy should be supported by appropriate incentives, performance metrics, and recognition systems that encourage adherence to the policy and reinforce the desired cultural attributes.

Aligning your AI Corporate Compliance Policy with

organizational objectives and culture is essential for creating a cohesive, supportive environment that facilitates responsible AI deployment and drives business success. By ensuring that your policy supports your organization's strategic goals and reinforces its core values, you can foster a culture of AI compliance that is integral to the achievement of long-term success in the age of AI.

ESTABLISHING MECHANISMS FOR STAKEHOLDER FEEDBACK AND POLICY REFINEMENT: ENSURING CONTINUOUS IMPROVEMENT AND ADAPTABILITY

An essential aspect of a successful AI Corporate Compliance Policy is the establishment of mechanisms for stakeholder feedback and policy refinement. By creating avenues for input from various stakeholders and continuously improving the policy based on their feedback, organizations can ensure that their AI compliance efforts remain effective, adaptable, and aligned with evolving needs, technologies, and regulations. In this section, we will discuss the importance of establishing mechanisms for stakeholder feedback and policy refinement, and provide guidance on how organizations can implement these mechanisms effectively.

Stakeholder feedback is invaluable for identifying areas of improvement, emerging risks, and new opportunities in the AI compliance landscape. By engaging with stakeholders such as employees, customers, partners, regulators, and industry experts, organizations can gain diverse perspectives on the effectiveness of their AI Corporate Compliance Policy and identify areas where the policy may need to be refined or updated.

To establish effective mechanisms for stakeholder feedback, organizations should create channels for communication and input, such as regular meetings, surveys, suggestion boxes, or online forums. These channels should be accessible, inclusive, and transparent, allowing stakeholders to share their feedback in a safe and constructive manner.

In addition to gathering stakeholder feedback, organizations should establish processes for reviewing and analyzing the input received, prioritizing the most critical issues and opportunities for improvement. This may involve creating a dedicated AI compliance committee or working group responsible for reviewing stakeholder feedback, identifying trends and patterns, and proposing refinements to the AI Corporate Compliance Policy.

Once refinements have been proposed, organizations should ensure that they are integrated into the policy in a timely and efficient manner. This may involve updating the policy document, communicating the changes to employees and stakeholders, and adjusting relevant processes, practices, and decision-making procedures accordingly.

Finally, organizations should continuously monitor the effectiveness of the refined policy and gather ongoing stakeholder feedback to ensure that the policy remains up-to-date, relevant, and responsive to the evolving AI compliance landscape.

Establishing mechanisms for stakeholder feedback and policy refinement is crucial for ensuring that your organization's AI Corporate Compliance Policy remains effective, adaptable, and aligned with evolving needs, technologies, and regulations. By creating avenues for input from various stakeholders and continuously improving the policy based on their feedback, organizations can foster a culture of AI compliance that drives long-term success in the age of AI.

FINAL THOUGHTS

As we conclude this chapter, it is important to recognize that crafting and implementing a robust AI Corporate Compliance Policy is an ongoing journey that requires continuous improvement, adaptability, and collaboration. The rapidly evolving landscape of AI technologies, regulations, and ethical considerations demands that organizations remain vigilant, proactive, and responsive to change in order to maintain responsible AI deployment and ensure long-term success.

A key takeaway from this chapter is the importance of engaging stakeholders from across the organization in the development, implementation, and refinement of the AI Corporate Compliance Policy. By fostering a culture of collaboration and inclusivity, organizations can harness the diverse perspectives, expertise, and insights of their stakeholders, driving more effective and comprehensive AI compliance efforts.

Moreover, organizations should embrace the principles of continuous improvement and adaptability in their AI compliance management, regularly reviewing and refining their policies based on stakeholder feedback, emerging risks, and evolving technologies and regulations. By committing to ongoing learning and growth, organizations can stay ahead of the curve and ensure that their AI initiatives remain responsible, ethical, and aligned with their strategic objectives and values.

As we navigate the complexities of AI compliance management, it is crucial for organizations to embrace a proactive, collaborative, and adaptive approach. By fostering a culture of continuous improvement and collaboration, organizations can ensure that their AI Corporate Compliance Policies remain effective, relevant, and responsive to the ever-changing AI landscape, driving long-term success and responsible innovation in the age of AI.

CHAPTER 4

IMPLEMENTING AND ENFORCING THE AI CORPORATE COMPLIANCE POLICY: TURNING PLANS INTO ACTIONS AND ACHIEVING COMPLIANCE GOALS

DEVELOPING AN EFFECTIVE AI CORPORATE COMPLIANCE Policy is only the first step in ensuring responsible AI deployment within an organization. The real challenge lies in implementing and enforcing the policy, translating plans and intentions into tangible actions that drive compliance adherence and foster a culture of responsible AI innovation. In this section, we will discuss the critical aspects of implementing and enforcing an AI Corporate Compliance Policy, and provide guidance on how organizations can ensure that their policies are effectively put into practice.

The successful implementation and enforcement of an AI Corporate Compliance Policy require a coordinated and strategic approach that involves clear communication, well-defined roles and responsibilities, robust monitoring and reporting mechanisms, and a commitment to continuous improvement. By taking a structured and proactive approach to policy implementation and enforcement, organizations can effectively manage AI compliance risks, adhere to legal and ethical requirements, and enhance trust among stakeholders, including employees, customers, partners, and regulators.

In the upcoming sections, we will delve deeper into the various aspects of implementing and enforcing an AI Corporate Compliance Policy, exploring best practices and practical strategies that organizations can adopt to ensure that their compliance efforts translate into meaningful, sustainable results. By understanding and addressing the challenges and opportunities associated with policy implementation and enforcement, organizations can set the stage for responsible AI deployment and drive long-term success in the age of AI.

COMMUNICATING THE POLICY TO EMPLOYEES AND STAKEHOLDERS: ENSURING AWARENESS AND BUY-IN FOR SUCCESSFUL AI COMPLIANCE MANAGEMENT

Effective communication is a cornerstone of successful AI Corporate Compliance Policy implementation. It is crucial to ensure that employees and stakeholders are well-informed about the policy, its objectives, and their roles and responsibilities in achieving compliance. Raising awareness among employees and stakeholders about the organization's commitment to responsible AI deployment and the specific requirements and expectations outlined in the policy is crucial for driving buy-in and fostering a culture of compliance within the organization. Additionally, effective communication ensures that employees and stakeholders understand their roles and responsibilities in achieving AI compliance, enabling them to take appropriate actions and make informed decisions. Finally, open and transparent communication helps build trust among stakeholders, demonstrating the organization's dedication to ethical AI practices and accountability.

To effectively communicate the AI Corporate Compliance Policy, organizations should develop a comprehensive communication plan that includes clear and concise messaging, utilizing a variety of communication channels and formats to reach a diverse audience. This ensures that employees and stakeholders can access and engage with the policy in the way that best suits their needs and preferences. Targeted communication efforts should be directed towards specific stakeholder groups, addressing their unique concerns, interests, and responsibilities related to AI compliance. This targeted approach helps ensure that stakeholders feel heard and valued, and that they understand the specific implications of the policy for their roles and activities.

Establishing a regular cadence of communication around the AI Corporate Compliance Policy, providing updates on policy changes, compliance achievements, and emerging trends and challenges is essential for maintaining

awareness and engagement among employees and stakeholders. This ongoing communication reinforces the organization's commitment to continuous improvement in AI
compliance management.

Effective communication of the AI Corporate Compliance Policy is critical for raising awareness, driving buy-in,
and ensuring successful policy implementation. By developing a comprehensive communication strategy that
includes clear messaging, multiple channels and formats,
targeted communication, and ongoing updates, organizations can foster a culture of AI compliance and build trust
among employees and stakeholders.

Establishing Roles and Responsibilities for Compliance:
Building an Accountable and Collaborative Compliance
Infrastructure

A key aspect of successfully implementing and enforcing
an AI Corporate Compliance Policy is the clear definition
of roles and responsibilities for compliance within the organization. This ensures that all employees and stakeholders
understand their part in adhering to the policy and maintaining a culture of responsible AI innovation. In this
section, we will discuss the importance of establishing roles
and responsibilities for compliance and provide guidance on
how organizations can develop a structured and accountable
compliance infrastructure.

Clearly defining roles and responsibilities for compliance
has several benefits. First, it promotes accountability within
the organization by outlining the specific duties and expec-

tations associated with AI compliance for each stakeholder. This helps employees and stakeholders understand the scope of their responsibilities and the consequences of non-compliance. Second, it fosters a collaborative approach to AI compliance, encouraging cross-functional teamwork and communication to address complex AI-related challenges and opportunities. Finally, it streamlines compliance management and reporting by creating a clear chain of command and delineating the flow of information between different levels and functions within the organization.

To establish roles and responsibilities for AI compliance, organizations should consider the following steps:

- Identify key stakeholders: Determine the various individuals and departments within the organization that play a role in AI compliance, including senior leadership, AI project teams, legal, IT, HR, and other relevant departments.
- Define specific roles and responsibilities: For each stakeholder, outline the specific duties and expectations related to AI compliance, taking into account their unique expertise, resources, and position within the organization.
- Establish a governance structure: Create a clear governance structure for AI compliance, including decision-making authority, escalation processes, and reporting lines. This structure should be designed to facilitate efficient

communication, collaboration, and oversight of compliance efforts across the organization.

- Communicate expectations and provide support: Ensure that all stakeholders are aware of their roles and responsibilities for AI compliance and provide them with the necessary training, resources, and support to effectively fulfill their duties.
- Monitor performance and enforce accountability: Establish mechanisms for monitoring stakeholder performance in meeting AI compliance responsibilities, and enforce accountability through appropriate consequences for non-compliance, such as performance reviews, disciplinary action, or retraining.

Establishing clear roles and responsibilities for AI compliance is essential for building an accountable and collaborative compliance infrastructure within the organization. By identifying key stakeholders, defining specific duties and expectations, and creating a robust governance structure, organizations can effectively manage AI compliance risks, foster cross-functional collaboration, and ensure that all employees and stakeholders contribute to responsible AI innovation.

Developing Monitoring and Reporting Mechanisms: Ensuring Effective Oversight and Continuous Improvement in AI Compliance

An essential component of a robust AI Corporate Compliance Policy is the establishment of effective monitoring and reporting mechanisms. These mechanisms enable organizations to track progress, identify potential issues, and ensure adherence to AI compliance requirements. In this section, we will discuss the importance of developing monitoring and reporting mechanisms for AI compliance and provide guidance on how organizations can implement these systems to support continuous improvement in AI compliance management.

Developing monitoring and reporting mechanisms for AI compliance offers several benefits. First, it allows organizations to proactively identify and address potential compliance issues before they escalate into more significant problems. This early detection can help minimize the risk of regulatory penalties, reputational damage, and other negative consequences associated with non-compliance. Second, it facilitates data-driven decision-making by providing organizations with insights into the effectiveness of their AI compliance efforts, helping them identify areas for improvement and allocate resources more efficiently. Finally, it promotes transparency and accountability by demonstrating the organization's commitment to responsible AI innovation and enabling stakeholders to track progress and evaluate performance against AI compliance goals.

To develop effective monitoring and reporting mechanisms for AI compliance, organizations should consider the following steps:

Establish key performance indicators (KPIs): Identify the key metrics and indicators that will be used to measure compliance with the AI Corporate Compliance Policy. These KPIs should be aligned with the organization's AI strategy, goals, and specific compliance requirements, and should include both quantitative and qualitative measures.

- Implement monitoring tools and processes: Develop and deploy monitoring tools and processes to collect data on AI compliance KPIs. These tools may include AI-enabled monitoring systems, manual audits, or a combination of both, depending on the organization's needs and resources.

- Define reporting processes and standards: Establish processes and standards for reporting AI compliance data to relevant stakeholders, including senior leadership, regulators, and other external parties as required. This may involve developing reporting templates, guidelines, and schedules to ensure consistency and timeliness in reporting.

- Conduct regular reviews and updates: Periodically review and update monitoring and reporting mechanisms to ensure they remain relevant and effective in the face of changing AI technologies, regulations, and organizational objectives. This may involve refining KPIs, updating monitoring tools, or modifying reporting processes based on lessons learned and best practices.
- Foster a culture of continuous improvement: Encourage employees and stakeholders to actively engage in the monitoring and reporting process, soliciting feedback and suggestions for improvement, and fostering a culture of learning and continuous improvement in AI compliance management.

Developing effective monitoring and reporting mechanisms is critical for ensuring effective oversight and continuous improvement in AI compliance. By establishing relevant KPIs, implementing monitoring tools and processes, defining reporting standards, conducting regular reviews, and fostering a culture of continuous improvement, organizations can proactively manage AI compliance risks and demonstrate their commitment to responsible AI innovation.

Ensuring Continuous Improvement and Policy Updates: Adapting to Evolving AI Technologies and Regulatory Landscapes

The rapidly evolving landscape of artificial intelligence presents both opportunities and challenges for organizations. To keep pace with these changes and ensure compliance with relevant regulations and best practices, it is essential for organizations to adopt a proactive approach to AI compliance management. One key aspect of this approach is fostering continuous improvement and regularly updating AI Corporate Compliance Policies. By staying abreast of emerging AI technologies, regulatory changes, and industry best practices, organizations can effectively adapt their compliance policies to align with current trends and challenges.

Periodic reviews and assessments of AI Corporate Compliance Policies are crucial for identifying areas for improvement and ensuring their ongoing relevance. Engaging employees, stakeholders, and external partners in the continuous improvement process helps to ensure a comprehensive and well-rounded approach to AI compliance management. By incorporating diverse perspectives, organizations can more effectively address emerging risks and opportunities.

Updating policies and procedures based on the findings from reviews, assessments, and stakeholder feedback ensures that organizations maintain effective and relevant AI compliance strategies. Communicating any updates or changes to employees and stakeholders is essential for fostering awareness and understanding of new requirements and expectations. Providing appropriate training and support helps to ensure that all members of the organization can effectively contribute to AI compliance efforts.

Finally, measuring and tracking progress using key performance indicators (KPIs) and monitoring mechanisms enables organizations to evaluate the impact of policy updates and continuous improvement efforts. By using these insights to further refine and enhance their AI Corporate Compliance Policies, organizations can maintain a proactive approach to AI compliance management and successfully navigate the rapidly changing world of artificial intelligence.

FINAL THOUGHTS

Implementing and enforcing a comprehensive AI Corporate Compliance Policy is an essential component of responsible AI innovation within organizations. By adopting a proactive approach to AI compliance management, organizations can effectively mitigate risks, adhere to regulatory requirements, and seize new opportunities in the rapidly evolving world of artificial intelligence. This chapter provided insights and guidance on communicating AI compliance policies to employees and stakeholders, establishing roles and responsibilities, developing monitoring and reporting mechanisms, and ensuring continuous improvement and policy updates.

As the world of AI continues to advance and transform industries, organizations must remain agile and adaptable in their AI compliance efforts. By fostering a culture of compliance, engaging stakeholders across the organization, and staying abreast of emerging trends and developments, organizations can successfully navigate the complex landscape of AI compliance and drive responsible innovation. Ultimately, a well-crafted and effectively implemented AI Corporate Compliance Policy serves as a foundation for organizational success in the age of artificial intelligence, promoting ethical decision-making, risk management, and sustainable growth.

CHAPTER 5

FOSTERING A CULTURE OF AI COMPLIANCE FOR RESPONSIBLE INNOVATION

ESTABLISHING A CULTURE OF AI COMPLIANCE WITHIN AN organization is a critical aspect of successfully managing the potential risks and ethical considerations associated with artificial intelligence. A strong compliance culture not only supports adherence to regulatory requirements and industry best practices but also promotes responsible innovation and sustainable growth. This chapter will explore the key components of building a culture of AI compliance, including fostering awareness and commitment among employees, encouraging ethical AI decision-making, and integrating AI compliance into the organization's core values and culture. By embracing a proactive and collaborative approach to AI compliance management, organizations can effectively navigate the complex landscape of AI-driven innovation while ensuring ethical and responsible business practices.

FOSTERING AWARENESS AND COMMITMENT AMONG EMPLOYEES: EMPOWERING THE WORKFORCE FOR AI COMPLIANCE SUCCESS

Creating a strong culture of AI compliance within an organization requires fostering awareness and commitment among employees at all levels. By equipping employees with the knowledge and understanding of AI compliance requirements and best practices, organizations can empower their workforce to contribute effectively to AI compliance efforts and ensure the successful implementation of AI Corporate Compliance Policies.

To promote awareness and commitment, organizations should focus on providing comprehensive training and educational programs that cover key aspects of AI compliance, including regulatory requirements, ethical considerations, and organizational policies. These training programs should be tailored to the specific needs and roles of employees, ensuring that each individual has the necessary knowledge and skills to contribute to AI compliance efforts in their area of responsibility.

In addition to formal training programs, organizations can foster employee awareness and commitment by promoting a culture of open communication and collaboration. Encouraging employees to engage in discussions about AI compliance issues, share their insights and experiences, and contribute to the ongoing development and refinement of AI compliance policies and procedures can help create a sense of collective ownership and responsibility.

Moreover, recognizing and rewarding employee efforts in AI compliance can further enhance commitment and drive a culture of compliance within the organization. By acknowledging the contributions of employees who demonstrate exemplary compliance behavior or identify potential compliance risks, organizations can motivate their workforce to remain vigilant and proactive in their AI compliance efforts.

Ultimately, fostering awareness and commitment among employees is a crucial component of building a culture of AI compliance that supports responsible innovation and ensures adherence to ethical standards and regulatory requirements.

Encouraging Ethical AI Decision-Making: Promoting Responsible Innovation and Sustainable Growth

One of the key components of building a culture of AI compliance is encouraging ethical decision-making in the development and deployment of artificial intelligence solutions. By prioritizing ethical considerations and fostering a sense of collective responsibility, organizations can effectively mitigate potential risks associated with AI-driven innovation and ensure sustainable growth.

To encourage ethical AI decision-making, organizations should first establish a clear set of ethical principles and guidelines that align with their overall business values and objectives. These principles should be embedded in the organization's AI Corporate Compliance Policy and communicated effectively to employees at all levels. Providing practical guidance on how to apply these principles in day-to-day decision-making can help employees understand the ethical implications of their actions and make more informed choices.

In addition, organizations should promote a culture of transparency and accountability when it comes to AI decision-making. By fostering open communication and collaboration across different teams and departments, organizations can facilitate the sharing of ideas, insights, and best practices that contribute to more ethical AI outcomes. Encouraging employees to challenge assumptions, question the status quo, and raise concerns about potential ethical risks can help ensure that AI-driven innovation is guided by a strong ethical compass.

Furthermore, organizations should provide employees with the necessary tools and resources to support ethical AI decision-making. This may include access to expert guidance, relevant literature, and industry best practices, as well as opportunities for professional development and continuous learning. Providing a supportive environment in which employees can grow their understanding of AI ethics and compliance can empower them to make more responsible choices in their work.

By encouraging ethical AI decision-making, organizations can create a culture of AI compliance that not only adheres to regulatory requirements and industry standards but also fosters responsible innovation and contributes to long-term business success.

INTEGRATING AI COMPLIANCE INTO ORGANIZATIONAL CULTURE: CREATING A FOUNDATION FOR RESPONSIBLE INNOVATION AND SUCCESS

Successfully building a culture of AI compliance requires the integration of compliance principles and practices into the very fabric of an organization's culture. By making AI compliance a core component of the organization's values, beliefs, and norms, businesses can ensure that ethical AI decision-making and adherence to regulatory requirements become second nature for all employees.

To integrate AI compliance into the organizational culture, leadership must play a critical role in setting the tone and direction for the entire organization. Top management should consistently demonstrate their commitment to AI compliance by actively participating in compliance initiatives, allocating resources to support compliance efforts, and communicating the importance of compliance to the organization's success.

Moreover, organizations should ensure that AI compliance is woven into the fabric of their day-to-day operations. This can be achieved by incorporating compliance considerations into decision-making processes, performance evaluations, and even employee onboarding and training programs. By making AI compliance a regular and expected part of employees' everyday activities, organizations can foster a shared understanding of the importance of compliance and create a sense of collective responsibility.

Another crucial aspect of integrating AI compliance into organizational culture is establishing clear channels for reporting and addressing compliance concerns. By providing employees with a safe and supportive environment to raise potential issues and seek guidance, organizations can create a culture of openness and accountability that encourages proactive compliance management.

Finally, organizations should continuously assess and refine their AI compliance efforts to ensure that they remain aligned with the organization's evolving needs and objectives. By regularly reviewing and updating their AI Corporate Compliance Policies, businesses can adapt to emerging technologies, regulations, and industry best practices, fostering a culture of continuous improvement and responsible innovation.

By integrating AI compliance into the very core of their organizational culture, companies can create a solid foundation for responsible AI-driven innovation, ensuring long-term business success and adherence to ethical standards and regulatory requirements.

REWARDING AND RECOGNIZING EMPLOYEES FOR AI COMPLIANCE ADHERENCE: ENCOURAGING A CULTURE OF RESPONSIBILITY AND COMMITMENT

Recognizing and rewarding employees for their adherence to AI compliance policies and ethical practices is a crucial aspect of building a culture of AI compliance within an organization. By celebrating the efforts and accomplishments of employees who demonstrate a commitment to responsible AI innovation, businesses can reinforce the importance of compliance and encourage a sense of shared responsibility among their workforce.

To effectively reward and recognize AI compliance adherence, organizations should establish clear and transparent criteria for evaluating employee performance in this area. These criteria should be closely aligned with the organization's AI Corporate Compliance Policy and may include factors such as proactive identification and mitigation of potential risks, effective communication of compliance concerns, and demonstrated commitment to ethical decision-making.

Organizations should also develop a range of reward and recognition mechanisms that cater to the diverse needs and preferences of their employees. This may include financial incentives, such as bonuses or promotions, as well as non-financial rewards, such as public recognition, additional training opportunities, or increased responsibility. By offering a variety of rewards and recognition options, organizations can ensure that their employees feel valued and appreciated for their compliance efforts.

In addition to formal reward and recognition programs, organizations should also foster a culture of informal recognition and support for AI compliance adherence. This may involve creating opportunities for employees to share their compliance successes and best practices with their colleagues or encouraging managers to provide regular feedback and recognition for compliance-related achievements.

Finally, it is important for organizations to regularly evaluate the effectiveness of their reward and recognition programs in promoting AI compliance adherence. By gathering feedback from employees and analyzing the impact of these programs on compliance outcomes, businesses can identify areas for improvement and refine their strategies to better support and motivate their workforce.

By rewarding and recognizing employees for their adherence to AI compliance policies and ethical practices, organizations can create a supportive environment that encourages responsibility, commitment, and innovation, ultimately contributing to long-term business success and ethical AI deployment.

FINAL THOUGHTS

As we conclude this chapter on building a culture of AI compliance, it is essential to recognize the critical role that organizational culture plays in driving responsible AI innovation and long-term business success. By fostering awareness, commitment, and ethical decision-making among employees, organizations can create a supportive environment that promotes adherence to AI compliance policies and regulatory requirements.

Throughout this chapter, we have emphasized the importance of leadership involvement, employee recognition and rewards, and the integration of AI compliance into day-to-day operations as key strategies for cultivating a culture of AI compliance. These efforts should be underpinned by clear communication, continuous learning, and ongoing evaluation to ensure that organizations remain agile and responsive to the evolving landscape of AI compliance.

In the end, building a culture of AI compliance is not a one-time initiative but rather an ongoing process that requires sustained effort and commitment from all levels of the organization. By actively engaging employees, celebrating their successes, and providing them with the tools and support they need to navigate the complexities of AI compliance, organizations can lay the foundation for a future of responsible innovation, regulatory adherence, and long-term business success.

As we move forward through the remaining chapters of

this book, we will continue to explore the various aspects of AI Corporate Compliance Policies, providing insights, strategies, and best practices to help organizations effectively navigate the challenges and opportunities presented by AI-driven innovation.

CHAPTER 6

NAVIGATING LEGAL AND ETHICAL CONSIDERATIONS IN AI DEPLOYMENT: BALANCING INNOVATION AND RESPONSIBILITY

As artificial intelligence (AI) continues to transform the business landscape, organizations must navigate a complex web of legal and ethical considerations to ensure responsible and compliant AI deployment. In this chapter, we will explore the various legal and ethical challenges that organizations face when implementing AI solutions, providing guidance and insights to help businesses balance the need for innovation with their commitment to responsible AI practices.

AI deployment brings with it a unique set of concerns, ranging from data privacy and protection to fairness, transparency, and accountability. These issues are often intertwined and may present conflicting priorities, requiring organizations to make difficult decisions as they strive to create AI-driven solutions that are both innovative and compliant with ethical and regulatory standards.

To successfully navigate these legal and ethical considerations, organizations must develop a deep understanding of the relevant laws, regulations, and industry best practices, as well as the potential risks and consequences associated with AI deployment. This knowledge will enable businesses to create AI Corporate Compliance Policies that effectively address the various challenges they face, supporting informed decision-making and minimizing the potential for negative impacts on their customers, stakeholders, and society at large.

In the following sections, we will delve deeper into the key legal and ethical considerations in AI deployment, offering practical guidance and recommendations to help organizations create a strong foundation for responsible AI innovation. By addressing these challenges proactively and systematically, businesses can not only mitigate potential risks but also unlock the full potential of AI to drive long-term success and competitive advantage.

DATA PRIVACY AND PROTECTION: SAFEGUARDING SENSITIVE INFORMATION IN THE AGE OF AI

Data privacy and protection have become increasingly critical concerns as businesses increasingly rely on AI-driven solutions to gain insights, make predictions, and drive decision-making. AI systems often require large volumes of data to function effectively, which can include sensitive personal information, raising questions about how this data is collected, stored, and processed. In this section, we will discuss the importance of data privacy and protection in AI deployment and provide guidance on how organizations can safeguard sensitive information while still leveraging the full potential of AI technologies.

One of the first steps in addressing data privacy and protection in AI deployment is understanding the various laws and regulations that govern these issues, such as the General Data Protection Regulation (GDPR) in the European Union or the California Consumer Privacy Act (CCPA) in the United States. These regulations impose strict requirements on organizations when it comes to the handling of personal data, including obtaining user consent, ensuring data security, and providing transparency around data processing activities.

To comply with these regulations and protect the privacy of individuals, organizations should implement robust data governance frameworks that outline clear policies and procedures for the collection, storage, and processing of personal information. This includes conducting data privacy impact assessments (DPIAs) to identify potential risks, adopting privacy-by-design principles, and implementing strong encryption and access controls to prevent unauthorized access or data breaches.

In addition to legal compliance, businesses must also consider the ethical implications of data privacy and protection in AI deployment. This involves being transparent about the use of personal data, respecting user privacy rights, and considering the potential consequences of AI-driven decisions on individuals and communities. By adopting a holistic approach that balances innovation with the need for privacy and protection, organizations can create AI-driven solutions that deliver value while also safeguarding the trust and confidence of their customers, stakeholders, and the wider society.

Bias Mitigation and Fairness: Ensuring Equitable Outcomes in AI-driven Decision-making

As AI systems become increasingly prevalent in various industries, the issue of bias mitigation and fairness has emerged as a critical concern. AI algorithms often learn from historical data, which can contain biases that inadvertently lead to unfair or discriminatory outcomes in decision-making processes. Addressing these issues is essential not only to meet ethical and legal requirements but also to ensure that organizations maintain trust with their customers and stakeholders. In this section, we will explore strategies for mitigating bias and promoting fairness in AI-driven decision-making.

Identifying and addressing biases in AI systems is a complex, ongoing process that requires collaboration across multiple functions within an organization. To begin, businesses should conduct thorough audits of their AI models to detect potential biases, both in the input data and in the algorithms themselves. This includes examining the quality and representativeness of training data, understanding the assumptions and limitations of the AI model, and assessing the potential impacts of algorithmic decisions on different demographic groups.

Once biases are identified, organizations can implement various techniques to mitigate their effects. These may include re-sampling or re-weighting the training data to ensure a more balanced representation, using techniques such as adversarial training or fair representation learning to reduce bias in the AI model, and employing interpretable models to enhance transparency and enable bias detection.

In addition to technical solutions, fostering a culture of fairness within the organization is vital. This involves raising awareness of potential biases among employees, particularly those involved in AI development and deployment, and promoting collaboration between data scientists, ethicists, and other stakeholders to address these issues holistically.

Moreover, organizations should establish clear guidelines and metrics for fairness, incorporating them into their AI Corporate Compliance Policies. By regularly monitoring and evaluating the performance of AI systems against these fairness metrics, businesses can identify areas for improvement and ensure continuous progress towards more equitable outcomes.

Ultimately, addressing bias and promoting fairness in

AI-driven decision-making is a multifaceted challenge that requires both technical and organizational solutions. By embracing this challenge and proactively working to mitigate biases, businesses can create AI systems that not only drive innovation but also contribute to a more just and inclusive society.

TRANSPARENCY AND EXPLAINABILITY: DEMYSTIFYING AI DECISION-MAKING FOR STAKEHOLDERS

In the era of AI-driven decision-making, transparency and explainability are crucial for establishing trust and accountability. As AI systems become more complex and integrated into critical decision-making processes, it is increasingly important for organizations to ensure that these systems are not only accurate and efficient but also understandable and explainable to stakeholders. In this section, we will discuss the importance of transparency and explainability in AI decision-making and outline strategies for achieving these goals within your organization's AI Corporate Compliance Policies.

Transparency refers to the openness and accessibility of information about an AI system's functionality, data sources, and decision-making processes. Ensuring transparency allows stakeholders, such as employees, customers, and regulators, to gain insight into the workings of AI systems and better understand the rationale behind their outputs. This, in turn, enables organizations to establish trust and credibility, minimize potential risks and liabilities, and comply with legal and ethical requirements.

Explainability, on the other hand, focuses on making the logic and reasoning behind AI-driven decisions understandable to humans. This involves breaking down complex algorithms and models into more interpretable and digestible formats. Explainability is essential for empowering stakeholders to evaluate AI decisions, identify potential biases or errors, and provide feedback for improvement.

To achieve transparency and explainability, organizations can adopt several strategies. First, invest in the development and deployment of interpretable AI models, which are designed to provide insights into their internal workings and decision-making processes. This may involve using simpler models or incorporating explainability techniques, such as Local Interpretable Model-agnostic Explanations (LIME) or Shapley Additive Explanations (SHAP).

Second, establish clear communication channels and documentation practices to convey information about AI systems to stakeholders. This includes creating user-friendly explanations of AI models and their decision-making processes, disclosing data sources and any potential biases, and providing guidelines for using AI-driven outputs responsibly.

Lastly, involve stakeholders in the development and evaluation of AI systems. Solicit input from diverse groups, including employees, customers, and regulators, to ensure that AI-driven decisions are aligned with stakeholder expectations and values. By involving stakeholders in the AI decision-making process, organizations can foster trust, promote collaboration, and ensure that AI systems are designed and deployed ethically and responsibly.

Transparency and explainability are essential components of responsible AI deployment. By integrating these principles into your organization's AI Corporate Compliance Policies, you can establish trust, accountability, and credibility with stakeholders while minimizing potential risks and liabilities associated with AI-driven decision-making.

ACCOUNTABILITY AND RESPONSIBILITY: ENSURING AI SYSTEMS ALIGN WITH ORGANIZATIONAL VALUES AND STANDARDS

As organizations increasingly rely on AI systems to inform decisions and automate processes, it becomes crucial to establish clear lines of accountability and responsibility for the development, deployment, and management of these systems. In this section, we will explore the importance of assigning accountability and responsibility in AI governance and provide recommendations for incorporating these principles into your AI Corporate Compliance Policies.

Accountability in the context of AI refers to the need to attribute the consequences of AI-driven decisions and actions to individuals or entities within the organization. As AI systems continue to shape critical decisions in various domains, it is essential to establish a robust framework to hold individuals and teams responsible for the development, deployment, and ongoing maintenance of these systems. This ensures that organizations can promptly address any issues, biases, or unintended consequences that may arise from AI-driven decisions, thus safeguarding the organization's reputation, legal standing, and ethical commitments.

Responsibility, on the other hand, pertains to the proactive ownership of AI-related tasks and outcomes by individuals or entities within the organization. This involves ensuring that the AI systems align with organizational objectives, values, and ethical principles, as well as conform to relevant industry regulations and requirements. Establishing clear lines of responsibility also fosters a culture of ethical AI decision-making and empowers stakeholders to take corrective actions when needed.

To embed accountability and responsibility in your AI Corporate Compliance Policies, consider the following recommendations:

- Clearly define roles and responsibilities within the organization for AI development, deployment, and management. This may include designating specific teams or individuals to oversee AI initiatives, as well as specifying their tasks and obligations in relation to AI governance.

- Implement a system of checks and balances to ensure that AI-driven decisions and actions are subject to review and scrutiny by relevant stakeholders. This may involve establishing mechanisms for regular audits, performance evaluations, and feedback loops to assess the effectiveness and ethical alignment of AI systems.
- Create a transparent and accessible reporting structure for AI-related concerns and issues. Encourage employees and stakeholders to report any concerns they may have about AI-driven decisions or the performance of AI systems, and ensure that there are clear channels and processes for addressing these concerns.
- Foster a culture of ongoing learning and improvement by regularly reviewing and updating AI Corporate Compliance Policies in light of new insights, technological advancements, and regulatory developments. This includes staying informed about emerging best practices and industry standards for AI governance and adapting your policies accordingly.

By establishing clear lines of accountability and responsibility for AI systems, organizations can ensure that their AI initiatives are developed and managed ethically and in

accordance with relevant legal and regulatory requirements. By embedding these principles into your AI Corporate Compliance Policies, you can create a robust
governance framework that promotes responsible innovation and mitigates potential risks associated with AI
deployment.

GLOBAL REGULATORY CONSIDERATIONS AND NAVIGATING INTERNATIONAL LAWS: A GUIDE TO AI COMPLIANCE IN A GLOBAL CONTEXT

As AI systems continue to drive innovation across industries
and markets, organizations increasingly need to navigate the
complex landscape of international laws and regulations
related to AI governance. In this section, we will discuss the
challenges of global regulatory compliance and offer guidance on how organizations can effectively address these
challenges within their AI Corporate Compliance Policies.

Operating in a global context, businesses must consider
the diverse legal frameworks and regulatory requirements
that govern AI deployment across different jurisdictions.
This can be particularly challenging given the rapidly
evolving nature of AI-related laws and the varying levels of
regulation in different countries. To ensure compliance with
international laws and regulations, organizations should
adopt a proactive and informed approach to their AI
Corporate Compliance Policies.

Here are some key strategies for navigating global regulatory considerations and international laws in your AI Corporate Compliance Policies:

- Stay informed about the latest developments in AI-related laws and regulations in the countries where your organization operates or intends to operate. This includes monitoring updates from regulatory authorities, participating in industry forums, and consulting with legal experts to keep abreast of emerging trends and requirements.
- Develop a flexible and adaptable policy framework that can accommodate the nuances of different legal and regulatory environments. This may involve creating modular policy components that can be customized to align with specific jurisdictional requirements, as well as incorporating mechanisms for regular policy updates and revisions as regulations evolve.
- Establish clear lines of responsibility for ensuring compliance with international laws and regulations within your organization. This may involve designating specific individuals or teams to oversee regulatory compliance across different jurisdictions and providing them with the necessary resources and support to fulfill their responsibilities.
- Collaborate with local partners and stakeholders to gain insights into local regulatory

requirements and best practices. This can help your organization better understand the specific legal and cultural contexts in which it operates and identify potential areas of improvement or risk mitigation in its AI Corporate Compliance Policies.

- Engage with international organizations, industry associations, and regulatory authorities to stay informed about emerging global standards and best practices for AI governance. By actively participating in these forums, your organization can contribute to the development of AI-related policies and standards that promote responsible innovation and cross-border collaboration.

In conclusion, navigating global regulatory considerations and international laws is a critical aspect of effective AI governance in a global context. By adopting a proactive and informed approach to AI Corporate Compliance Policies, organizations can better manage the complexities of international regulations and ensure that their AI initiatives are developed and managed in accordance with the highest ethical, legal, and industry standards.

Final Thoughts

In this chapter, we have explored the various legal and ethical considerations that organizations must address in the deployment of AI systems. From data privacy and protection to bias mitigation, transparency, explainability, and accountability, it is evident that AI compliance requires a comprehensive understanding of these complex issues and a proactive approach to integrating them into AI Corporate Compliance Policies.

As we have discussed, AI governance is not only about adhering to laws and regulations, but also about fostering a culture of responsible innovation within an organization. By implementing robust AI compliance measures, companies can ensure that their AI initiatives are developed and managed in accordance with the highest ethical, legal, and industry standards.

To successfully navigate these legal and ethical considerations, organizations should invest in building a solid foundation of knowledge and expertise in AI compliance. This includes staying informed about the latest developments in AI-related laws and regulations, engaging with industry experts and stakeholders, and actively participating in the development of global standards and best practices for AI governance.

Moreover, organizations should ensure that their AI Corporate Compliance Policies are flexible and adaptable to the rapidly evolving landscape of AI governance. By creating a policy framework that can accommodate the nuances of different legal and regulatory environments, organizations can better manage the complexities of international regulations and ensure that their AI initiatives are developed and managed in accordance with the highest ethical, legal, and industry standards.

Navigating legal and ethical considerations in AI deployment is a critical aspect of effective AI governance. By embracing a proactive and informed approach to AI Corporate Compliance Policies, organizations can successfully manage these complexities and drive responsible innovation, paving the way for sustainable growth and long-term success in the AI-driven era.

CHAPTER 7

AI COMPLIANCE RISK ASSESSMENT AND MANAGEMENT

AS THE ADOPTION OF ARTIFICIAL INTELLIGENCE (AI) technologies accelerates across industries, the need for robust AI compliance risk assessment and management practices has become increasingly critical. This chapter delves into the essential components of AI compliance risk assessment and management, providing organizations with a comprehensive understanding of the processes and strategies necessary to ensure the responsible and ethical deployment of AI systems.

AI compliance risks can arise from various factors, such as data privacy breaches, biased algorithms, or a lack of transparency and explainability in AI decision-making processes. By proactively identifying and addressing these risks, organizations can mitigate potential adverse impacts on their stakeholders, reputation, and bottom line. Moreover, a robust AI risk management framework can help companies stay ahead of emerging regulations and maintain a competitive edge in the ever-evolving AI landscape.

In the following sections, we will discuss the steps involved in identifying and categorizing AI-related risks, conducting AI risk assessments, prioritizing risk mitigation efforts, and implementing effective risk management strategies for AI compliance. By integrating these practices into their AI Corporate Compliance Policies, organizations can foster a culture of responsible innovation and ensure the long-term success of their AI initiatives.

IDENTIFYING AND CATEGORIZING AI-RELATED RISKS

One of the foundational steps in AI compliance risk assessment and management is the identification and categorization of AI-related risks. By understanding the diverse range of risks associated with AI technologies, organizations can develop targeted strategies to address them and prioritize their mitigation efforts effectively.

AI-related risks can be broadly categorized into four main areas:

1. Data Risks: Data risks stem from issues related to data quality, privacy, security, and storage. These risks may include inadequate data protection measures, unauthorized access to sensitive

information, or inaccurate and biased data used to train AI models, leading to biased or unfair outcomes.

2. Technical Risks: Technical risks involve the performance, reliability, and security of AI systems. These may encompass system failures, vulnerabilities to cyberattacks, or the unintended consequences of AI algorithms, such as the amplification of harmful content or the generation of misleading information.

3. Ethical and Legal Risks: Ethical and legal risks arise from the potential violation of ethical principles, regulations, or laws related to AI deployment. Examples include discrimination resulting from biased algorithms, non-compliance with data protection regulations, or the lack of transparency and explainability in AI decision-making processes.

4. Operational and Reputational Risks: Operational and reputational risks pertain to the potential negative impacts of AI deployment on an organization's operations, reputation, or stakeholder relationships. These risks can materialize as a result of inadequate AI governance structures, insufficient employee training and awareness, or negative public perception of the organization's AI practices.

By systematically identifying and categorizing the various AI-related risks, organizations can create a comprehensive inventory of potential threats and challenges. This inventory serves as the basis for conducting AI risk assessments, prioritizing risk mitigation efforts, and developing targeted risk management strategies for AI compliance.

CONDUCTING AI RISK ASSESSMENTS AND PRIORITIZING RISK MITIGATION

Conducting AI risk assessments is an essential step in the AI compliance process, as it enables organizations to understand the magnitude and likelihood of AI-related risks and prioritize their mitigation efforts accordingly. A robust risk assessment process involves the following key steps:

1. Establish a Risk Assessment Framework: Develop a consistent and repeatable framework for assessing AI-related risks, which includes defining risk criteria, establishing risk rating scales, and setting risk tolerance thresholds. This framework should be aligned with the organization's overall risk management approach and integrate with existing processes and tools.

2. Assess Risk Severity and Likelihood: Using the risk inventory created during the identification and categorization phase, evaluate the severity and likelihood of each identified risk. Severity

refers to the potential impact of the risk on the organization's objectives, while likelihood represents the probability of the risk materializing. This assessment should consider both quantitative and qualitative factors, and involve input from relevant stakeholders, such as legal, IT, and HR departments.

3. Prioritize Risks for Mitigation: Based on the assessed severity and likelihood, prioritize the identified risks for mitigation efforts. This prioritization process should take into account the organization's risk tolerance levels, as well as any legal, regulatory, or industry requirements. High-priority risks should be addressed first, followed by medium and low-priority risks.

4. Develop Risk Mitigation Strategies: For each prioritized risk, develop targeted risk mitigation strategies to reduce its likelihood, minimize its impact, or both. These strategies may include implementing technical controls, revising policies and procedures, enhancing employee training, or improving monitoring and reporting mechanisms. Ensure that the selected strategies align with the organization's AI compliance objectives and resource constraints.

5. Monitor and Review Risk Assessments: Regularly monitor the effectiveness of risk mitigation strategies and update risk assessments

as necessary to reflect changes in the AI landscape, regulatory environment, or the organization's objectives. This continuous monitoring and review process allows organizations to adapt their risk management approach in response to emerging risks and evolving compliance requirements.

By conducting thorough AI risk assessments and prioritizing risk mitigation efforts, organizations can proactively manage AI-related risks and enhance their overall AI compliance posture. This proactive approach not only helps to prevent potential regulatory violations and reputational damage but also supports responsible innovation and long-term business success.

IMPLEMENTING RISK MANAGEMENT STRATEGIES FOR AI COMPLIANCE

The successful implementation of risk management strategies for AI compliance requires a structured, systematic approach that involves collaboration across various organizational functions. This section outlines the key steps involved in implementing AI risk management strategies to ensure compliance and mitigate potential adverse consequences.

1. Assign Ownership and Responsibility: Start by designating specific individuals or teams with the responsibility for overseeing the implementation of each AI risk mitigation strategy. This may involve creating new roles, such as an AI compliance officer or AI risk manager, or assigning responsibilities to existing teams within the organization. Clearly define the roles and responsibilities of these individuals or teams, and ensure they have the necessary authority, resources, and support to execute their tasks effectively.

2. Develop a Detailed Implementation Plan: Create a comprehensive plan that outlines the specific actions required to implement each risk mitigation strategy. This plan should include clear objectives, timelines, and performance indicators, as well as the necessary resources and budget allocations. Where appropriate, break down the plan into manageable tasks and milestones to facilitate progress tracking and accountability.

3. Provide Training and Support: Ensure that all relevant employees receive appropriate training and support to enable them to understand and adhere to the AI compliance policies and procedures. This may involve providing targeted training on AI ethics, data privacy, and other

relevant topics, as well as offering ongoing support through helpdesks, workshops, or other resources.

4. Implement Monitoring and Reporting Mechanisms: Establish robust monitoring and reporting mechanisms to track the effectiveness of risk mitigation strategies and to identify any emerging risks or compliance issues. These mechanisms may include regular audits, real-time monitoring of AI systems, and periodic reporting to senior management or regulatory authorities. Leverage data analytics and AI-powered tools, where possible, to enhance monitoring capabilities and identify trends or patterns that may signal potential compliance risks.

5. Review and Adapt Strategies: Periodically review and assess the effectiveness of the implemented risk management strategies to ensure they remain relevant and effective in addressing the evolving AI risk landscape. Identify any gaps or areas for improvement and revise the strategies as needed. This may involve updating policies, enhancing monitoring mechanisms, or providing additional training and support to employees.

By following these steps, organizations can effectively implement AI risk management strategies that not only help them to comply with relevant regulations and ethical guidelines but also support responsible innovation and long-term business success. Establishing a culture of continuous improvement and adaptation is key to navigating the dynamic and rapidly changing world of AI compliance.

Final Thoughts

In today's increasingly digitized world, artificial intelligence (AI) has become an integral component of business innovation and growth. However, with the potential benefits of AI come significant risks and challenges that must be effectively managed to ensure compliance with legal and ethical standards. This chapter has provided a comprehensive overview of the key components of AI compliance, including risk assessment, management, and mitigation strategies.

By embracing a proactive and systematic approach to AI compliance, organizations can not only safeguard their operations from potential legal and ethical pitfalls but also foster a culture of responsible innovation. A strong commitment to AI compliance can help organizations cultivate trust among customers, employees, and regulators, ultimately contributing to long-term business success and competitive advantage.

As the AI landscape continues to evolve, it is crucial for organizations to remain agile and adaptable in their approach to AI compliance. Regularly reviewing and updating AI policies, investing in employee training and development, and staying abreast of new regulations and industry best practices are all essential components of a robust and sustainable AI compliance strategy.

The successful integration of AI technologies into business processes requires a careful balance between innovation and compliance. By investing in the development and implementation of comprehensive AI compliance policies and practices, organizations can confidently navigate the complexities of the AI era and harness the full potential of this transformative technology for sustainable growth and success.

CHAPTER 8

AI COMPLIANCE TRAINING AND EDUCATION PROGRAMS: EMPOWERING YOUR WORKFORCE FOR RESPONSIBLE AI DEPLOYMENT

THE RAPID EVOLUTION AND ADOPTION OF ARTIFICIAL intelligence (AI) in businesses have transformed the way organizations operate and interact with customers, stakeholders, and the wider public. As AI technologies continue to permeate various industries, it is becoming increasingly important for organizations to ensure that their workforce is equipped with the knowledge and skills required to effectively manage the associated risks and adhere to the highest standards of ethical and legal compliance. To this end, AI Compliance Training and Education Programs have emerged as essential components of a comprehensive corporate compliance strategy.

In this section, we will explore the importance of AI compliance training and education programs, the key elements of an effective training curriculum, and the various methods and resources available to help organizations build a workforce that is well-versed in the principles, guidelines, and best practices of responsible AI deployment. By investing in the continuous education and professional development of employees, organizations can create a strong culture of AI compliance and ensure that their AI systems are used responsibly, ethically, and in accordance with the law.

DESIGNING EFFECTIVE AI COMPLIANCE TRAINING FOR EMPLOYEES: BUILDING A COMPETENT AND ETHICALLY-MINDED WORKFORCE

An essential aspect of fostering a culture of AI compliance within an organization is to provide employees with the necessary training and educational resources to ensure that they understand and adhere to relevant policies, regulations, and ethical standards. Designing an effective AI compliance training program requires a well-thought-out and structured approach that addresses the unique needs and objectives of the organization, as well as the diverse roles and responsibilities of its employees.

To begin with, it is important to identify the target audience for the training program. This will typically include employees who are directly involved in the development, deployment, and management of AI systems, as well as those who interact with or are affected by these systems in their day-to-day work. Additionally, management and leadership should also be included in the training process to ensure that they are aware of their responsibilities in overseeing AI compliance and fostering a culture of ethical AI decision-making.

Next, the training content should be tailored to the specific requirements of the organization and the industry it operates in, taking into account any relevant regulations, guidelines, and best practices. The curriculum should cover key areas such as data privacy and protection, bias mitigation and fairness, transparency and explainability, accountability, and navigating international laws and regulations. It is crucial to strike a balance between technical knowledge and ethical considerations, as both are essential components of AI compliance.

Furthermore, the training program should utilize a combination of learning methodologies and resources, such as classroom-style lectures, interactive workshops, case studies, online courses, and expert-led seminars. This will help ensure that employees with different learning preferences and levels of expertise can effectively absorb and retain the information being presented.

Lastly, it is important to establish a system for tracking and evaluating the effectiveness of the training program. This may include periodic assessments, employee feedback, and performance reviews, as well as the identification of any gaps or areas of improvement in the training curriculum. By continuously refining the AI compliance training program, organizations can ensure that their workforce remains up-to-date with the latest developments and best practices in AI ethics and regulation.

EVALUATING THE IMPACT OF TRAINING PROGRAMS ON COMPLIANCE ADHERENCE: MEASURING SUCCESS AND ENSURING CONTINUOUS IMPROVEMENT

An essential component of any AI compliance training program is evaluating its impact on employees' understanding, adherence, and commitment to the established policies, regulations, and ethical guidelines. This not only helps organizations measure the effectiveness of their training initiatives, but also identifies areas for improvement and ensures that the training program remains relevant and up-to-date.

To evaluate the impact of AI compliance training, organizations should first establish clear objectives and key performance indicators (KPIs) that align with their overall compliance goals. These may include metrics such as the level of employee engagement, the extent of policy understanding, the rate of policy violations, and the number of successful AI system deployments adhering to ethical standards.

Next, organizations should implement various assessment tools to measure the extent to which these objectives are being met. Pre- and post-training tests can be used to gauge employees' understanding of the material and identify areas where additional training or resources may be needed. Surveys and feedback forms can help gather insights into employees' perceptions of the training program, as well as their level of confidence in applying the knowledge and skills learned.

Additionally, organizations should closely monitor their AI systems and processes to track compliance adherence. This may involve regular audits, incident reporting, and reviews of AI projects to ensure that the established policies and ethical guidelines are being followed. By tracking the rate of policy violations or non-compliant AI deployments, organizations can gain valuable insights into the effectiveness of their training initiatives and identify any gaps or shortcomings that need to be addressed.

Finally, it is important to foster a culture of continuous learning and improvement, which includes regularly reviewing and updating the training program to incorporate new developments, best practices, and lessons learned. This may involve collaborating with external experts, industry partners, and regulatory bodies to stay current with the latest advancements in AI ethics and regulation.

By systematically evaluating the impact of their AI compliance training programs, organizations can ensure that they are effectively preparing their workforce to navigate the complex landscape of AI ethics, regulation, and policy adherence, thereby reducing the risk of non-compliance and fostering a culture of responsible innovation.

Continuous Learning and Adapting Training to Evolving AI Compliance Needs: Embracing Change and Nurturing a Culture of Ongoing Improvement

AI technology is rapidly evolving, and with it, the ethical, legal, and regulatory landscape surrounding its deployment and use. This dynamic environment presents both opportunities and challenges for organizations striving to maintain a robust AI compliance program. To keep pace with these changes and ensure the ongoing effectiveness of their AI policies and training programs, organizations must prioritize continuous learning and adaptability.

Fostering a culture of continuous learning starts by recognizing that AI compliance training is not a one-time event, but rather an ongoing process that requires regular updates, review, and refinement. Organizations should stay informed about the latest developments in AI technology, ethical guidelines, and regulatory requirements by engaging with industry experts, participating in forums, attending conferences, and monitoring relevant publications and news sources.

As new knowledge and insights emerge, organizations should incorporate these findings into their AI compliance training programs, ensuring that employees are equipped with the most up-to-date understanding of the technology and its implications. This may involve updating training content, revising case studies, and introducing new tools and resources that facilitate learning and compliance adherence.

To support continuous learning, organizations should also create opportunities for employees to engage with AI compliance topics outside of formal training sessions. This can be achieved through activities such as lunch-and-learn sessions, webinars, workshops, and cross-functional team projects, which enable employees to deepen their understanding, share knowledge, and collaborate on AI-related challenges.

In addition to updating the training content, organizations should also periodically review their training delivery methods to ensure they remain engaging and effective. New technologies, such as e-learning platforms, virtual reality, and gamification, can help enhance the learning experience and improve the retention of knowledge.

By embracing continuous learning and adaptability, organizations can ensure that their AI compliance training programs remain relevant, engaging, and effective in the face of an ever-changing AI landscape. This not only helps organizations navigate the complexities of AI ethics and regulation, but also fosters a culture of responsible innovation and resilience in the face of change.

FINAL THOUGHTS

In this chapter, we have explored the essential components of designing, implementing, and evaluating effective AI compliance training and education programs. By investing in the development of comprehensive and dynamic training initiatives, organizations can not only equip their employees with the knowledge and skills necessary to navigate the complex landscape of AI ethics and regulation, but also foster a culture of responsible innovation and proactive risk management.

As AI technology continues to evolve and reshape the way we live and work, it is crucial that organizations prioritize AI compliance training and education as an integral part of their overall compliance strategy. By cultivating a proactive and forward-thinking approach, organizations can stay ahead of emerging risks, ensure alignment with legal and ethical requirements, and capitalize on the transformative potential of AI technology.

To achieve this, organizations must be willing to adapt and evolve their training programs in response to new developments, emerging best practices, and shifting regulatory landscapes. This requires a commitment to continuous learning, open dialogue, and collaboration across all levels of the organization.

AI compliance training and education is a vital element of any organization's AI compliance strategy. By fostering a culture of awareness, commitment, and continuous improvement, organizations can navigate the challenges and uncertainties associated with AI technology and harness its power to drive innovation, efficiency, and growth.

CHAPTER 9

THE POWER OF CROSS-FUNCTIONAL COLLABORATION FOR AI COMPLIANCE

As ORGANIZATIONS INCREASINGLY EMBRACE AI technologies to drive innovation, enhance efficiency, and create competitive advantages, ensuring compliance with legal, ethical, and regulatory requirements becomes a shared responsibility that cuts across all departments and business units. In this chapter, we delve into the vital role of cross-functional collaboration for AI compliance, and discuss the strategies and best practices that can help organizations to effectively manage the complex, interrelated challenges that arise from AI deployment.

Cross-functional collaboration is essential for organizations to develop a holistic understanding of the risks and opportunities associated with AI technologies and to create a robust, integrated AI compliance strategy. By fostering open communication and cooperation between different teams and stakeholders, organizations can harness the diverse perspectives, expertise, and experiences needed to navigate the rapidly evolving landscape of AI ethics and regulation. This collaborative approach enables organizations to proactively identify and address potential compliance issues, while also fostering a culture of shared responsibility and commitment to responsible AI innovation.

In the sections that follow, we will explore the key principles and practices for successful cross-functional collaboration in AI compliance, including the establishment of dedicated AI compliance committees, the promotion of interdisciplinary communication, and the creation of a shared vision and goals for AI technology deployment.

ENGAGING STAKEHOLDERS ACROSS THE ORGANIZATION IN AI COMPLIANCE EFFORTS

A key aspect of successful AI compliance management is the active engagement of stakeholders across the entire organization. By involving a diverse range of individuals and departments in AI compliance efforts, organizations can ensure that their strategies and policies are informed by a wide array of perspectives, experiences, and expertise. This holistic approach is essential for identifying and addressing the complex and interconnected challenges that arise from the deployment of AI technologies.

To effectively engage stakeholders in AI compliance efforts, organizations should first identify the key departments and individuals who have a direct or indirect influence on AI deployment and management. This may include, but is not limited to, IT, data management, human resources, legal, finance, marketing, and operations teams. Once the relevant stakeholders have been identified, organizations should establish clear communication channels and forums for collaboration, such as regular meetings, workshops, or working groups, where stakeholders can share insights, discuss challenges, and contribute to the development of AI compliance strategies and policies.

In addition to fostering collaboration and information sharing, organizations should also strive to empower stakeholders by providing them with the necessary resources, support, and training to effectively contribute to AI compliance efforts. This may involve offering targeted education and training programs, creating clear guidelines and frameworks for decision-making, and promoting a culture of open communication and mutual support.

By actively engaging stakeholders across the organization in AI compliance efforts, companies can ensure that their strategies and policies are comprehensive, effective, and well-aligned with the organization's broader goals and values. This, in turn, will help to mitigate risks, enhance trust, and promote responsible AI innovation.

COLLABORATING WITH LEGAL, IT, AND HR DEPARTMENTS TO ENSURE COMPREHENSIVE COMPLIANCE

To achieve comprehensive AI compliance, organizations must foster a culture of collaboration among key departments, particularly legal, IT, and human resources (HR). These departments play a critical role in ensuring that AI technologies are deployed responsibly, ethically, and in accordance with applicable laws and regulations.

Legal departments are responsible for staying up-to-date on relevant legal and regulatory requirements, as well as helping the organization navigate the complex landscape of AI-related laws and regulations. They must work closely with other departments to ensure that AI policies and practices align with these requirements, while also providing guidance on potential legal risks and liabilities associated with AI deployment.

IT departments, on the other hand, are responsible for managing the technical aspects of AI deployment, such as data management, infrastructure, and security. They must collaborate with legal and HR departments to ensure that AI systems are designed and implemented in a manner that complies with relevant data privacy and protection regulations. Additionally, IT departments must work with other stakeholders to establish robust monitoring and reporting mechanisms that can identify and address potential compliance issues in real-time.

HR departments play a crucial role in fostering a culture of AI compliance within the organization. This includes designing and implementing training and education programs to ensure that employees are aware of and adhere to AI compliance policies. HR departments must also work closely with legal and IT departments to establish clear guidelines, roles, and responsibilities for AI compliance management, as well as to develop policies and procedures for addressing AI-related misconduct or violations.

By fostering cross-functional collaboration between legal, IT, and HR departments, organizations can create a comprehensive and well-rounded AI compliance strategy that addresses the diverse challenges associated with AI deployment. This collaborative approach not only helps to mitigate risks and protect the organization from legal and reputational harm but also promotes responsible innovation and a culture of trust and accountability.

BUILDING INTERNAL PARTNERSHIPS TO FACILITATE AI COMPLIANCE MANAGEMENT

Cultivating strong internal partnerships is essential for effective AI compliance management. By establishing open lines of communication and cooperation among various departments and teams within an organization, businesses can ensure that AI technologies are deployed responsibly and ethically, while also adhering to applicable legal and regulatory requirements.

An essential starting point for building internal partnerships is to identify key stakeholders who will be directly involved in AI-related initiatives, such as members of the data science, engineering, product management, and business strategy teams. By involving these stakeholders in the development and implementation of AI compliance policies and procedures, organizations can create a more holistic and informed approach to AI compliance management.

Collaboration among stakeholders should not be limited to only those teams directly involved in AI initiatives. For example, the marketing and sales departments can provide valuable insights into the potential ethical implications of AI systems, as they often have a deep understanding of customer expectations and needs. Likewise, the finance and procurement departments can help identify potential risks and liabilities associated with AI-related contracts and partnerships.

Encouraging open dialogue and regular meetings among stakeholders can facilitate the sharing of knowledge, expertise, and best practices, while also promoting a culture of mutual support and understanding. This collaborative approach to AI compliance management can lead to more effective decision-making and risk mitigation strategies, as well as increased organizational agility and adaptability in the face of evolving AI-related challenges.

In addition to fostering internal partnerships, organizations should also consider engaging with external partners, such as industry associations, academic institutions, and regulatory bodies, to stay abreast of the latest developments in AI compliance and best practices. By actively participating in relevant networks and communities, organizations can contribute to the broader conversation on AI ethics and regulation, while also gaining valuable insights and resources to support their own AI compliance efforts.

FINAL THOUGHTS

cross-functional collaboration is an integral aspect of building a robust AI compliance program within an organization. By fostering strong internal partnerships and actively engaging with External stakeholders, businesses can effectively navigate the complex landscape of AI ethics, regulation, and risk management. This collaborative approach not only helps organizations to ensure that they adhere to AI compliance policies and best practices, but also promotes a culture of responsibility, innovation, and shared ownership in the deployment and use of AI technologies.

As the field of AI continues to evolve at a rapid pace, organizations must remain agile and adaptive to stay ahead of emerging compliance challenges and capitalize on the many opportunities that AI presents. By investing in open communication, collaboration, and continuous learning, businesses can build a solid foundation for AI compliance management that supports their strategic objectives and fosters long-term success in an increasingly AI-driven world.

CHAPTER 10

AI COMPLIANCE AUDITING AND REPORTING

AI COMPLIANCE AUDITING AND REPORTING PLAY A CRITICAL role in maintaining an organization's adherence to established policies, regulations, and ethical standards. Regular audits enable businesses to evaluate the effectiveness of their AI compliance programs, identify potential areas of concern, and take corrective action to mitigate risks and ensure ongoing compliance.

The process of AI compliance auditing involves a comprehensive assessment of an organization's AI systems, processes, and controls. This includes evaluating the adherence to data privacy and protection standards, examining the fairness and bias mitigation measures employed, and assessing the transparency and explainability of AI algorithms. Additionally, audits must consider the organization's compliance with relevant industry regulations, as well as its approach to AI risk management and mitigation strategies.

To ensure a thorough and unbiased audit, organizations should engage independent external auditors or consultants with expertise in AI compliance. These professionals can provide valuable insights and recommendations for improving the organization's compliance posture, while also ensuring the highest level of objectivity and impartiality in the auditing process.

AI compliance reporting is another essential aspect of maintaining an effective compliance program. Regular reporting enables organizations to track their progress in meeting compliance objectives and demonstrate their commitment to responsible AI deployment. Reports should be shared with relevant stakeholders, including senior management, board members, and regulators, to maintain transparency and foster accountability.

Organizations must establish robust mechanisms for AI compliance reporting, which may include automated monitoring tools, regular status updates, and periodic reviews. By integrating AI compliance auditing and reporting into their overall compliance management framework, businesses can continuously refine and enhance their AI systems, policies, and practices, ensuring that they remain aligned with evolving ethical and regulatory requirements.

ESTABLISHING PROCESSES FOR PERIODIC INTERNAL AND EXTERNAL AUDITS

Periodic internal and external audits are vital for ensuring the ongoing effectiveness of an organization's AI compliance program. These audits provide valuable insights into the strengths and weaknesses of a company's AI systems, policies, and practices, helping to identify areas of concern and opportunities for improvement. To establish a robust audit process, organizations must consider the following key elements:

1. Setting audit frequency and scope: Determine the appropriate frequency and scope for internal and external audits, based on factors such as the size and complexity of the organization, the nature and risk level of its AI systems, and relevant regulatory requirements. Audits should be conducted at regular intervals, with the flexibility to adjust the schedule as needed to address emerging risks or changes in the AI landscape.

2. Developing an audit plan: Outline a comprehensive audit plan that includes objectives, scope, methodology, and key deliverables. This plan should provide a clear roadmap for conducting the audit, ensuring that all relevant aspects of the organization's AI compliance program are assessed thoroughly and systematically.

3. Engaging skilled auditors: Assemble a team of skilled

internal auditors who possess the necessary expertise in AI compliance, data privacy, and industry-specific regulations. For external audits, select a reputable, independent firm with a proven track record in AI compliance auditing to provide an objective and impartial assessment.

4. Conducting the audit: Execute the audit plan, evaluating the organization's AI systems, processes, and controls against the established compliance policies and regulatory requirements. Ensure that the audit team has access to all relevant documentation and personnel to facilitate a comprehensive assessment.

5. Documenting findings and recommendations: Prepare a detailed audit report that outlines the findings, highlights areas of concern, and provides actionable recommendations for improvement. This report should serve as a basis for informed decision-making and strategic planning to enhance the organization's AI compliance program.

6. Communicating results and implementing changes: Share the audit results with relevant stakeholders, including senior management, board members, and regulators. Develop an action plan to address identified gaps and implement recommended changes, leveraging cross-functional collaboration to ensure a successful execution.

By establishing processes for periodic internal and external audits, organizations can proactively monitor and improve their AI compliance programs, reducing risks and fostering a culture of responsible AI deployment.

DEVELOPING AI COMPLIANCE REPORTING STANDARDS AND TEMPLATES

Establishing clear and consistent AI compliance reporting standards and templates is crucial for organizations to effectively communicate their AI-related activities, progress, and challenges to stakeholders, regulators, and the wider public. These reporting tools provide transparency and accountability, while also demonstrating a company's commitment to responsible AI deployment. To develop effective AI compliance reporting standards and templates, organizations should consider the following guidelines:

1. Align with existing standards and frameworks: Leverage existing industry standards, regulatory guidelines, and AI ethics frameworks to ensure that the reporting standards and templates are comprehensive, relevant, and up-to-date. This alignment can help organizations avoid duplicative efforts and streamline their reporting process.

2. Define reporting scope and frequency: Determine the appropriate scope and frequency for AI compliance reporting, taking into account factors such as the organization's size, industry, risk profile, and regulatory environment. Establish clear expectations around when, how, and to whom the reports will be submitted.

3. Develop clear and concise templates: Create standardized templates that capture essential information related to AI compliance in a clear, concise, and easily digestible format.

The templates should cover key aspects such as AI system descriptions, data privacy practices, bias mitigation efforts, transparency measures, and accountability mechanisms.

4. Include qualitative and quantitative metrics: Incorporate both qualitative and quantitative metrics in the reporting templates to provide a comprehensive view of the organization's AI compliance efforts. This can include performance indicators, benchmarks, and targets that help stakeholders assess the progress and effectiveness of the AI compliance program.

5. Encourage consistency and comparability: Develop reporting standards that promote consistency and comparability across different AI systems, departments, and organizations. This can help stakeholders to more easily understand and compare AI compliance efforts, fostering industry-wide best practices and collaboration.

6. Provide guidance and training: Offer guidance and training to employees on the proper use of the reporting standards and templates, ensuring that they understand the importance of accurate, timely, and consistent AI compliance reporting. This can help build a culture of accountability and transparency within the organization.

7. Regularly review and update standards and templates: Conduct periodic reviews of the reporting standards and templates to ensure that they remain relevant, effective, and aligned with the evolving AI landscape and regulatory requirements. Solicit feedback from stakeholders to identify areas for improvement and incorporate updates as needed.

By developing robust AI compliance reporting standards and templates, organizations can foster transparency, accountability, and trust in their AI systems, while also demonstrating their commitment to ethical AI deployment and fostering a culture of AI compliance.

UTILIZING AUDIT FINDINGS TO REFINE AND IMPROVE AI CORPORATE COMPLIANCE POLICIES

Leveraging audit findings is an essential step in refining and improving AI corporate compliance policies. It allows organizations to identify areas of weakness, address potential risks, and ensure that their policies remain up-to-date, effective, and aligned with regulatory requirements. The following paragraphs outline key considerations for utilizing audit findings to enhance AI compliance policies:

1. Analyze and prioritize findings: Begin by thoroughly analyzing the audit findings to identify patterns, trends, and areas of concern. Prioritize the findings based on their impact, urgency, and the organization's risk tolerance. This helps in focusing resources on addressing the most critical issues first.

2. Identify root causes and areas for improvement: For each identified issue, determine the root cause and assess how the current AI compliance policy may have contributed to the problem. This may involve examining policy gaps, lack of clarity, or inadequate enforcement mechanisms. By under-

standing the underlying causes, organizations can develop targeted solutions for improvement.

3. Develop and implement action plans: Create detailed action plans to address the identified issues and areas for improvement. The plans should include specific steps, responsibilities, and timelines for completion. This helps ensure accountability and timely execution of the necessary changes.

4. Communicate changes to stakeholders: Keep stakeholders informed about the audit findings and the resulting changes to the AI compliance policy. Clear communication promotes transparency, builds trust, and encourages ongoing engagement in the compliance process.

5. Update training and education programs: As the AI compliance policy evolves, it is crucial to update the organization's training and education programs accordingly. This ensures that employees are well-equipped to adhere to the revised policy and fosters a culture of ongoing learning and AI compliance awareness.

6. Monitor progress and effectiveness: Regularly monitor the progress of the action plans and assess the effectiveness of the implemented changes. This can be achieved through ongoing compliance reporting, periodic reviews, and additional audits as needed. Monitoring helps to identify any emerging issues and enables organizations to respond proactively to new challenges.

7. Foster a culture of continuous improvement: Encourage a

mindset of continuous improvement within the organization, emphasizing the importance of learning from audit findings and making iterative enhancements to the AI compliance policy. This approach enables organizations to stay ahead of the curve in the ever-evolving AI landscape and maintain a robust, effective compliance program.

By utilizing audit findings to refine and improve their AI corporate compliance policies, organizations can ensure that their policies remain effective, mitigate risks, and demonstrate their commitment to responsible AI deployment. Additionally, this proactive approach fosters a culture of continuous improvement and collaboration, driving the organization towards AI compliance excellence.

ENGAGING THIRD-PARTY AUDITORS FOR UNBIASED ASSESSMENTS

In the realm of AI compliance, engaging third-party auditors can provide valuable unbiased assessments of an organization's AI policies and practices. Third-party audits offer an impartial perspective on the effectiveness of an organization's AI compliance program, helping to identify potential areas of improvement and validating the organization's commitment to ethical AI deployment.

External auditors possess extensive experience and expertise in evaluating AI compliance programs, often drawing on best practices and benchmarking against industry standards. This allows them to provide insightful recommendations that may not be apparent to an organization's internal compliance team. Furthermore, external auditors are not influenced by internal politics or biases, leading to a more objective evaluation.

The benefits of engaging third-party auditors for AI compliance assessments include increased credibility and transparency. By voluntarily subjecting their AI compliance programs to external scrutiny, organizations demonstrate to their stakeholders, including customers, regulators, and investors, that they take their AI compliance obligations seriously. This can help build trust and confidence in the organization's AI systems and practices.

When selecting a third-party auditor, it is essential to consider factors such as their reputation, experience, and expertise in the field of AI compliance. Additionally, it is crucial to establish a clear scope of work, outlining the specific areas to be audited and the desired outcomes of the engagement. This ensures that both parties are aligned on expectations and objectives, leading to a more fruitful and effective audit process.

Engaging third-party auditors for unbiased assessments of AI compliance programs offers numerous benefits for organizations. It provides an impartial evaluation of the organization's AI policies and practices, identifies areas for improvement, and demonstrates a commitment to ethical AI deployment. By partnering with external auditors, organizations can continually refine their AI compliance programs and ensure that they remain at the forefront of responsible AI innovation.

FINAL THOUGHTS

In this chapter, we have explored various aspects of AI compliance auditing and reporting, emphasizing the importance of these processes in maintaining a robust and effective AI compliance program. Establishing processes for periodic internal and external audits, developing AI compliance reporting standards and templates, utilizing audit findings to refine and improve AI Corporate Compliance Policies, and engaging third-party auditors for unbiased assessments are all crucial components of a comprehensive AI compliance strategy.

By implementing these measures, organizations can ensure that they stay up to date with evolving legal and ethical requirements, while continuously improving their AI policies and practices. This not only demonstrates a strong commitment to ethical AI deployment but also helps build trust with stakeholders, including customers, regulators, and investors.

As AI technologies continue to advance and permeate various industries, the need for a robust AI compliance program will only become more critical. Organizations that invest in comprehensive auditing and reporting processes will be better equipped to navigate the complex landscape of AI compliance, ultimately driving responsible innovation and success in the age of AI.

Chapter 11

AI Compliance in Mergers, Acquisitions, and Partnerships: Introduction

As AI technologies become increasingly integral to business operations across various industries, their role in mergers, acquisitions, and partnerships has also become a significant consideration. In this chapter, we will explore the challenges and opportunities that arise when incorporating AI compliance into the decision-making process for mergers, acquisitions, and partnerships. By understanding the importance of AI compliance in these transactions, organizations can better assess potential risks, align their AI policies and practices with their strategic objectives, and ultimately foster responsible innovation through collaboration.

ASSESSING AI COMPLIANCE IN TARGET COMPANIES DURING MERGERS AND ACQUISITIONS

In mergers and acquisitions, it is crucial for acquiring organizations to thoroughly assess the AI compliance of target companies to avoid potential legal, financial, and reputational risks. This evaluation process should involve a careful examination of the target company's AI policies, practices, and infrastructure, as well as its adherence to relevant regulations and ethical guidelines. Key aspects to consider include data privacy and protection, algorithmic fairness and bias mitigation, transparency, and explainability. By conducting a comprehensive assessment of AI compliance in target companies, acquiring organizations can identify potential issues, plan for integration, and ensure a smooth transition that aligns with their overall AI strategy and objectives.

ENSURING AI COMPLIANCE IN STRATEGIC PARTNERSHIPS AND COLLABORATIONS

When entering into strategic partnerships and collaborations, it is vital for organizations to ensure AI compliance across all involved parties. This process begins with a thorough evaluation of potential partners' AI policies, practices, and track records, with a focus on their adherence to relevant regulations and ethical guidelines. By clearly defining the roles and responsibilities of each party in terms of AI compliance, organizations can establish a strong foundation for collaboration. Additionally, it is essential to develop shared guidelines, standards, and processes for AI development and deployment, along with mechanisms for communication, monitoring, and reporting on AI compliance. By taking these steps, organizations can foster a collaborative environment that promotes innovation while maintaining a strong commitment to ethical and responsible AI practices.

INTEGRATING AI CORPORATE COMPLIANCE POLICIES ACROSS MERGED ORGANIZATIONS

When two or more organizations merge, it is crucial to ensure a smooth and effective integration of AI Corporate Compliance Policies. This process requires a comprehensive understanding of the individual policies, practices, and systems of each organization. A successful integration strategy involves identifying commonalities and differences between the existing policies and determining the most effective way to align them with the newly merged organization's objectives, culture, and risk appetite. This may involve adopting best practices from each organization, harmonizing policies, and addressing any gaps or discrepancies in compliance measures. It is essential to establish clear communication channels and involve stakeholders from both organizations in the decision-making process to ensure a smooth transition. By diligently integrating AI Corporate

Compliance Policies, merged organizations can create a cohesive, unified approach to managing AI-related risks and opportunities while maintaining compliance with legal and ethical requirements.

FINAL THOUGHTS

Navigating the complexities of AI compliance in mergers, acquisitions, and partnerships requires a thorough understanding of each organization's policies, practices, and systems. By carefully assessing AI compliance in target companies and ensuring compliance in strategic collaborations, organizations can minimize potential risks and maximize the value of their partnerships. Furthermore, the successful integration of AI Corporate Compliance Policies across merged organizations creates a unified approach to managing AI-related risks and opportunities, while remaining compliant with legal and ethical requirements. As the world of AI continues to evolve, it is vital for businesses to stay informed, agile, and proactive in their AI compliance efforts, ensuring that they remain at the forefront of innovation while upholding ethical standards and regulatory requirements.

CHAPTER 12

PREPARING FOR THE FUTURE OF AI COMPLIANCE

THE RAPID ADVANCEMENTS IN ARTIFICIAL INTELLIGENCE HAVE led to its increasing adoption across various industries, making it crucial for organizations to prepare for the future of AI compliance. As AI systems become more sophisticated and their applications more widespread, the regulatory landscape will continue to evolve, presenting new challenges and opportunities for businesses. In this chapter, we will discuss the importance of staying abreast of emerging trends and technologies, as well as the strategies organizations can employ to ensure their AI policies and compliance practices remain effective and adaptable in the face of continuous change. By fostering a proactive approach to AI compliance, organizations can effectively mitigate risks, seize opportunities, and remain at the forefront of innovation while upholding ethical standards and regulatory requirements.

ADAPTING TO EMERGING TECHNOLOGIES AND REGULATIONS

In the dynamic world of AI, organizations must be prepared to adapt to emerging technologies and changing regulations to maintain compliance and stay competitive. Staying informed about advancements in AI, such as new algorithms, applications, and tools, can help businesses anticipate the impact on their operations and make timely adjustments to their compliance policies. Furthermore, monitoring regulatory developments at the local, national, and international levels can provide valuable insights into potential shifts in the compliance landscape.

To effectively adapt to these changes, organizations should establish a dedicated team or designate individuals responsible for staying informed about AI-related technological and regulatory developments. Regular training and education programs can help employees stay up-to-date on new advancements and their implications for AI compliance. Additionally, fostering a culture of open communication and cross-functional collaboration can ensure that relevant information is shared and acted upon swiftly. By remaining agile and responsive to emerging technologies and regulations, organizations can better navigate the evolving AI compliance landscape, mitigate potential risks, and capitalize on new opportunities.

LEVERAGING AI TO ENHANCE COMPLIANCE MANAGEMENT

Harnessing the power of AI itself can be instrumental in
streamlining and improving compliance management within
organizations. AI-driven solutions can help automate
processes, identify trends, and even predict potential compliance issues before they escalate. By integrating AI into
compliance management efforts, organizations can achieve
increased efficiency, accuracy, and overall effectiveness.

AI-powered tools can be used to monitor large volumes
of data, identify patterns, and flag potential compliance
concerns, such as data privacy breaches or signs of bias in
decision-making. These tools can also aid in automating the
review and analysis of legal and regulatory documents,
enabling organizations to stay current with the latest
requirements and adapt their policies accordingly. AI-driven
analytics can further provide insights into employee behavior, allowing companies to tailor training programs and
target specific areas in need of improvement.

By embracing AI in compliance management, organizations can not only reduce the manual burden on their teams
but also improve the detection and mitigation of risks. As AI
continues to advance, its potential to revolutionize compliance management will only grow, providing businesses with

the opportunity to stay ahead of the curve and maintain a strong compliance posture.

COLLABORATING WITH INDUSTRY EXPERTS AND REGULATORS

Forging strong relationships with industry experts and regulators is essential for organizations seeking to remain at the forefront of AI compliance. By actively engaging with these stakeholders, businesses can benefit from their expertise, stay informed about regulatory changes, and even help shape future guidelines and standards.

Collaboration with industry experts, such as AI researchers, ethicists, and legal professionals, can provide invaluable insights into emerging trends and best practices in AI compliance. These experts can offer guidance on addressing complex ethical and legal challenges, ensuring that organizations navigate the rapidly evolving AI landscape with confidence.

Engaging with regulators is equally crucial, as it allows organizations to keep abreast of new legislation and policy updates that may impact their AI deployments. By participating in industry forums, roundtables, and public consultations, companies can contribute to the development of balanced, well-informed regulations that take into account both the opportunities and risks associated with AI.

Establishing a dialogue with both industry experts and regulators demonstrates an organization's commitment to responsible AI practices and helps to build trust among stakeholders. As the world of AI continues to evolve, proactive collaboration with these key players will ensure that organizations remain agile, adaptable, and prepared to address the AI compliance challenges of the future.

ENCOURAGING INNOVATION WHILE MAINTAINING COMPLIANCE STANDARDS

Fostering a culture of innovation is essential for organizations to stay competitive in today's fast-paced, technology-driven world. However, striking a balance between encouraging innovation and maintaining compliance standards can be challenging, particularly when it comes to AI deployment. It is crucial for organizations to develop strategies that allow them to harness the potential of AI while adhering to ethical principles and regulatory requirements.

Firstly, organizations should invest in creating a robust AI compliance policy that clearly defines the ethical and legal boundaries within which their AI initiatives should operate. By providing a solid framework for AI development, employees can confidently innovate while ensuring their projects remain compliant.

Secondly, organizations should establish cross-functional teams that bring together experts from different departments, such as IT, legal, HR, and data privacy. These teams can facilitate the sharing of knowledge, helping to identify potential compliance risks early in the development process and ensuring that innovative AI solutions adhere to established standards.

Education and training are vital in promoting innovation while maintaining compliance. Providing employees with the necessary resources and tools to understand AI compliance requirements will empower them to develop creative solutions that meet both ethical and legal expectations.

Lastly, organizations should cultivate an open and transparent environment where employees feel comfortable discussing the ethical implications and compliance challenges associated with AI projects. Encouraging open dialogue can lead to the identification of innovative approaches to addressing compliance concerns, helping to drive responsible AI development.

By incorporating these strategies, organizations can effectively foster a culture of innovation while maintaining the highest standards of AI compliance, ensuring that their AI initiatives drive value while upholding ethical and legal principles.

FINAL THOUGHTS

Preparing for the future of AI compliance is essential for organizations seeking to harness the power of AI while remaining accountable, ethical, and legally compliant. By adapting to emerging technologies and regulations, leveraging AI to enhance compliance management, collaborating with industry experts and regulators, and encouraging innovation within the bounds of compliance standards, organizations can effectively navigate the rapidly evolving landscape of AI compliance.

Developing a proactive approach to AI compliance will not only help organizations to mitigate risks and meet legal obligations, but also establish a strong reputation for ethical AI deployment. In turn, this will enable companies to build trust with their customers, partners, and regulators, providing a solid foundation for long-term success.

As AI continues to permeate every aspect of business and society, staying informed, agile, and responsive to the latest developments in AI compliance will become increasingly vital. By fostering a culture of continuous learning and improvement, organizations can ensure that they remain at the forefront of AI innovation while upholding the highest standards of ethics and compliance.

CHAPTER 13

CASE STUDIES - SUCCESSFUL AI CORPORATE COMPLIANCE POLICIES

In this chapter, we will delve into case studies that illustrate successful AI corporate compliance policies implemented by various organizations. These real-world examples will provide valuable insights into the practical application of the concepts and strategies discussed throughout the book. By examining the experiences of these organizations, readers can gain a deeper understanding of the challenges and opportunities that come with the adoption and management of AI compliance policies.

From tech giants to small and medium-sized enterprises, companies across industries have adopted AI technologies to drive innovation, streamline processes, and enhance decision-making. As AI applications become increasingly sophisticated and pervasive, it is crucial for organizations to ensure that their AI initiatives are aligned with ethical and legal standards. The following case studies will showcase the steps that these organizations have taken to establish robust AI compliance policies, offering valuable lessons and inspiration for others embarking on their own AI compliance journey.

EXAMPLES OF EFFECTIVE AI COMPLIANCE POLICIES IN VARIOUS INDUSTRIES

In this section, we will explore examples of effective AI compliance policies across diverse industries, demonstrating how these organizations have tailored their approaches to address the unique challenges and requirements of their respective sectors.

1. Healthcare: A major healthcare provider implemented an AI compliance policy to ensure that its AI-driven diagnostic tools meet data privacy and security regulations. The policy includes strict guidelines for data handling, regular audits to assess compliance with privacy laws, and ongoing training for employees on the ethical use of AI.
2. Finance: A global financial institution established an AI compliance policy to manage the risks associated with AI-driven decision-making in areas such as credit scoring and fraud detection. The policy emphasizes transparency, explainability, and fairness, and includes regular audits of AI models to ensure their unbiased performance.
3. Retail: A large retail chain has adopted an AI compliance

policy to govern the use of AI in customer analytics and inventory management. The policy outlines guidelines for data usage, privacy, and security, and mandates the integration of fairness and accountability measures in all AI-driven processes.

4. Manufacturing: An industrial manufacturer has put in place an AI compliance policy to manage the deployment of AI-powered automation and quality control systems. The policy focuses on safety and reliability, requiring rigorous testing and validation of AI systems, and establishes clear lines of responsibility for AI-related decisions and outcomes.

5. Public Sector: A government agency has developed an AI compliance policy to guide the use of AI in public services, such as traffic management and welfare distribution. The policy prioritizes transparency, accountability, and public engagement, and includes provisions for ongoing evaluations of AI systems to ensure their alignment with societal values and norms.

These examples illustrate the versatility and adaptability of AI compliance policies, demonstrating how organizations across various industries can develop tailored strategies to manage the legal, ethical, and practical challenges associated with AI deployment. By learning from these successful implementations, companies can design and execute AI compliance policies that not only safeguard their interests but also promote responsible AI adoption and innovation.

LESSONS LEARNED AND BEST PRACTICES

Drawing from the diverse case studies and experiences in AI compliance across various industries, this section highlights key lessons learned and best practices that can guide organizations in developing and implementing effective AI compliance policies.

1. Tailor AI compliance policies to industry-specific needs: Each industry faces unique challenges and opportunities related to AI deployment. It is crucial for organizations to develop AI compliance policies that address the specific requirements and risks of their industry while adhering to overarching legal and ethical principles.

2. Prioritize transparency and explainability: Ensuring that AI systems are transparent and explainable not only promotes trust among stakeholders but also enables organizations to monitor and evaluate the performance and ethical implications of their AI deployments more effectively.

3. Integrate fairness and bias mitigation measures: AI systems can unintentionally perpetuate biases and contribute to unfair outcomes. Organizations must incorporate fairness and bias mitigation strategies into their AI compliance policies to ensure equitable treatment of all stakeholders.

4. Establish clear lines of accountability and responsibility: AI compliance policies should outline the roles and responsibilities of individuals and teams within the organization.

This clarity helps to ensure that all stakeholders understand their obligations and can be held accountable for AI-related decisions and outcomes.

5. Implement continuous monitoring and improvement: AI compliance is not a one-time exercise. Organizations should establish processes for ongoing monitoring, assessment, and refinement of their AI compliance policies to adapt to evolving technologies, regulations, and industry best practices.

6. Foster cross-functional collaboration: AI compliance requires input and collaboration from various departments within an organization, including legal, IT, HR, and business units. Encouraging cross-functional collaboration helps to ensure that AI compliance policies are comprehensive, practical, and well-integrated into the organization's operations.

7. Invest in education and training: Regular training and education programs help employees stay informed about AI compliance requirements and best practices, enabling them to make responsible decisions when deploying and managing AI systems.

8. Engage with external stakeholders: Collaborating with industry experts, regulators, and other stakeholders can provide valuable insights and guidance on AI compliance best practices, emerging trends, and regulatory developments.

By incorporating these lessons learned and best practices into their AI compliance strategies, organizations can effectively manage the risks associated with AI deployment, promote responsible AI adoption, and position themselves for success in the rapidly evolving world of AI technology.

ADAPTING TO UNIQUE ORGANIZATIONAL CONTEXTS

In the realm of AI compliance, there is no one-size-fits-all solution. Each organization has its unique context, culture, objectives, and challenges that must be considered when developing and implementing an AI Corporate Compliance Policy. This section delves into the importance of adapting AI compliance strategies to an organization's specific context and offers insights on how to achieve this.

1. Understand the organization's mission and values: An effective AI compliance policy should align with the organization's mission and core values. By incorporating these principles into the policy, organizations can ensure that AI deployments are consistent with their strategic objectives and foster a culture of ethical AI use.
2. Assess the organization's AI maturity: Organizations should evaluate their current AI maturity level, considering factors such as the extent of AI adoption, in-house AI expertise, and existing compliance infrastructure. This assessment will inform the development of a tailored AI

compliance policy that addresses the organization's specific needs and challenges.

3. Consider the organization's size and structure: The size and structure of an organization can influence the complexity and scope of its AI compliance policy. Large organizations with multiple departments and business units may require more comprehensive policies, while smaller organizations may need more streamlined approaches. In both cases, it is essential to establish clear lines of responsibility and communication to ensure effective compliance management.

4. Engage stakeholders from diverse backgrounds: Inclusive stakeholder engagement can provide valuable insights into the unique aspects of an organization's context. By involving employees from various departments, levels of seniority, and backgrounds, organizations can identify potential blind spots, better understand the impact of AI deployments, and tailor compliance policies accordingly.

5. Customize training and education programs: AI compliance training should be customized to reflect the organization's specific context, industry, and AI maturity. By addressing the unique needs and concerns of employees, organizations can foster a culture of AI compliance that is both effective and sustainable.

6. Foster a culture of continuous improvement: As organizations evolve, so too should their AI compliance policies. By embracing a culture of continuous improvement, organizations can ensure that their AI compliance strategies remain

relevant and effective in the face of changing technologies, regulations, and organizational contexts.

By taking the time to understand their unique organizational context and adapting their AI compliance policies accordingly, organizations can develop robust, effective, and sustainable strategies that promote responsible AI adoption and mitigate associated risks.

ADDRESSING CHALLENGES AND OVERCOMING OBSTACLES IN IMPLEMENTING AI COMPLIANCE POLICIES

Implementing AI compliance policies is not without its challenges, as organizations face various obstacles in ensuring responsible and ethical AI adoption. This section outlines some of these challenges and offers practical solutions for overcoming them to create a robust AI compliance framework.

1. Navigating complex regulations: As AI technology evolves, so too does the regulatory landscape, which can be complex and fragmented. To navigate this dynamic environment, organizations should stay informed of the latest regulatory developments and consult with legal experts to ensure their policies are in line with current requirements.

2. Building internal expertise: Developing and maintaining AI compliance policies requires specialized knowledge and

expertise. Organizations can address this challenge by investing in training and upskilling their workforce, collaborating with external experts, and creating dedicated AI compliance roles.

3. Balancing innovation and compliance: Striking a balance between fostering innovation and adhering to compliance standards can be challenging. Organizations can address this by creating a culture of responsible innovation, ensuring that AI development and deployment are guided by ethical principles and compliance requirements.

4. Ensuring stakeholder buy-in: Gaining the support of stakeholders, such as employees, management, and investors, is essential for successful AI compliance policy implementation. Organizations can achieve this by clearly communicating the benefits of AI compliance, involving stakeholders in the policy development process, and fostering a culture of transparency and accountability.

5. Addressing resource constraints: Implementing AI compliance policies can be resource-intensive, particularly for smaller organizations. To overcome this challenge, organizations can leverage external resources, such as industry best practices, third-party tools, and consultants, to support their compliance efforts.

6. Overcoming resistance to change: As with any significant organizational shift, implementing AI compliance policies may face resistance from employees and other stakeholders. Organizations can address this by demonstrating the value

of AI compliance, providing training and support, and celebrating successes along the way.

By acknowledging the challenges and obstacles associated with implementing AI compliance policies, organizations can develop tailored strategies for overcoming them. This proactive approach enables organizations to create robust AI compliance frameworks that support responsible AI adoption and mitigate associated risks.

FINAL THOUGHTS

As we reach the conclusion of this book on AI policies and compliance, it is evident that the responsible adoption of artificial intelligence within corporations is no longer a luxury but a necessity. As AI continues to reshape the business landscape, organizations must embrace robust compliance frameworks to navigate the complex ethical, legal, and social implications that accompany these transformative technologies.

The journey towards AI compliance requires a proactive approach, fostering a culture of ethical decision-making and embedding compliance considerations into every stage of AI development and deployment. By prioritizing AI compliance, organizations can leverage the power of AI to drive innovation while safeguarding the rights and interests of stakeholders, including employees, customers, and society at large.

Through continuous learning, adaptation, and collaboration, organizations can stay ahead of the rapidly evolving AI compliance landscape, addressing emerging challenges and embracing new opportunities. By sharing best practices and lessons learned, we can collectively create a future where AI technologies are harnessed responsibly, ethically, and sustainably, to the benefit of all.

In closing, it is our hope that the insights and guidance provided in this book will serve as a valuable resource for corporations seeking to navigate the complex world of AI policies and compliance. As you embark on your own AI compliance journey, remember that the pursuit of responsible AI is not only a matter of compliance but also a commitment to building a better, more equitable future for all.

Conclusion

As we approach the final stretch of our journey through the complex world of AI policies and compliance, it is essential to recognize that the road to responsible AI is an ongoing and dynamic process. This concluding chapter will provide a comprehensive overview of the core principles, strategies, and best practices discussed throughout the book, highlighting the importance of continuous learning, adaptation, and collaboration in navigating the ever-evolving AI compliance landscape. By synthesizing the key takeaways, this chapter aims to serve as a valuable resource for corporations committed to embracing AI responsibly and ethically, ensuring the protection of stakeholders and the sustainable growth of their organizations.

The Importance of Proactive AI Compliance Management

In today's rapidly evolving technological landscape, adopting a proactive approach to AI compliance management is critical for corporations seeking to minimize risks and maintain their competitive edge. By actively anticipating and addressing potential legal, ethical, and operational challenges associated with AI deployment, organizations can not only safeguard their reputation and protect stakeholder interests but also foster an environment of innovation and responsible growth. Proactive AI compliance management involves continuous monitoring of emerging regulations, conducting regular risk assessments, and keeping abreast of industry best practices. Moreover, by fostering a culture of compliance, organizations can empower employees to make informed and ethical AI-related decisions, ultimately contributing to the long-term success and sustainability of the corporation.

The Role of AI Corporate Compliance Policies in Driving Business Success

AI Corporate Compliance Policies play a pivotal role in driving business success by ensuring that organizations harness the full potential of AI technologies while adhering to ethical, legal, and regulatory standards. Effective compliance policies create a robust framework that guides employees in the responsible deployment and management of AI systems, minimizing the risks associated with data privacy, security, and bias. By fostering a culture of transparency, accountability, and continuous improvement, these policies demonstrate a company's commitment to ethical AI practices, which can enhance brand reputation and contribute to increased customer trust. Furthermore, well-implemented compliance policies enable organizations to navigate the complex regulatory landscape, reducing the likelihood of costly fines, penalties, or legal actions. In essence, AI Corporate Compliance Policies lay the foundation for sustainable growth and innovation, enabling businesses to thrive in an increasingly competitive and AI-driven world.

FUTURE OUTLOOK AND POTENTIAL DEVELOPMENTS IN AI COMPLIANCE

As AI technologies continue to evolve and permeate various industries, the landscape of AI compliance will undoubtedly undergo significant transformations. Regulatory bodies and governments will likely introduce new laws and guidelines to address emerging concerns, such as AI-powered surveillance, deepfakes, and autonomous weaponry. Organizations must remain agile and adaptive to these changes, ensuring that their AI Corporate Compliance Policies reflect the most current legal and ethical requirements.

Additionally, we can anticipate the development of AI-driven compliance management tools that will streamline risk assessment, monitoring, and reporting processes. These solutions will not only enable organizations to maintain compliance more effectively but also provide valuable insights to refine and optimize AI systems. Cross-industry collaboration and knowledge-sharing will become increasingly important as organizations learn from one another's experiences and collectively establish best practices for responsible AI deployment.

Moreover, the growing emphasis on AI ethics and the societal impacts of these technologies will push businesses to prioritize fairness, transparency, and accountability in their AI applications. This focus will drive the need for interdisciplinary teams comprising data scientists, ethicists, and domain experts to collaborate on AI projects, ensuring that the systems developed are aligned with the organization's values and ethical standards.

In summary, the future of AI compliance will be marked by continuous evolution, innovation, and collaboration. Organizations that proactively adapt their compliance policies and invest in the necessary resources, tools, and training will be better positioned to navigate the challenges and seize the opportunities presented by AI-driven advancements.

ABOUT JAMIE CULICAN
AUTHOR, MARKETER, PUBLISHER, TEACHER

Jamie is a USA Today bestselling author with a passion for helping other authors succeed. She is the owner of Dragon Realm Press, a publishing house that specializes in working with indie authors. With over a decade of experience in the publishing industry, Jamie has become an expert in book marketing, book design, and book editing. Her approach is centered on creating a personalized and collaborative experience for her clients that results in high-quality, marketable books.

Her extensive marketing background allows her to guide authors through the complex world of book promotion, providing them with strategies that work. Jamie believes that every author has a unique voice, and she is committed to helping them share their stories with the world.

With a focus on innovation, Jamie has been at the forefront of integrating AI into the publishing industry. She believes that AI is a powerful tool that can help authors streamline their processes and reach new audiences. Jamie is passionate about helping authors navigate the ever-changing landscape of publishing and achieve their goals.

About Melle Melkumian
Author, Technologist, Marketer, Publisher

Melle has spent her career translating complex technology for the lay person, working with prestigious organizations such as NASA, Northrop Grumman, and Hewlett Packard. As the Marketing Director for an AI-enabled app company, Melle continues to leverage technology to drive meaningful change. She believes we are at a pivotal moment in history, where the incredible potential of AI is set to revolutionize the way we work and live. Melle is passionate about helping people navigate this shift and harness the power of AI to achieve their goals. Her expertise and unique perspective make her an invaluable resource for anyone looking to tap into the full potential of AI in their personal or professional life.

Outside of her professional career, Melle is a USA Today bestselling author, having published multiple books with rave reviews through a fresh approach to fantasy story-telling. Through her work as an author, Melle has gained a deep understanding of the writing and publishing process, and how emerging technologies like AI can support and enhance the creative process. She is excited to share her expertise and insights with fellow authors in the AI for Authors community.

About AI4CES
Empowering Professionals, Transforming Industries

AI4CES, the AI-focused educational platform designed to empower individuals across a wide range of vertical markets, including publishing, proposal and grant writing, and education. With our mission to make AI accessible to everyone, we provide comprehensive, tailored learning experiences through online classes, webinars, and more. Our expertly crafted courses break down complex AI concepts into digestible, easy-to-understand lessons, enabling you to harness the power of AI and revolutionize the way you work in your industry.

Don't miss the opportunity to stay ahead in today's competitive landscape by mastering AI with AI4CES. Our adaptive, engaging, and interactive learning modules ensure that you receive personalized, cutting-edge education in a format that suits your needs and preferences. Join the AI revolution with AI4CES and transform the way you approach challenges in your profession, from publishing to grant writing and beyond.

www.ai4ces.com